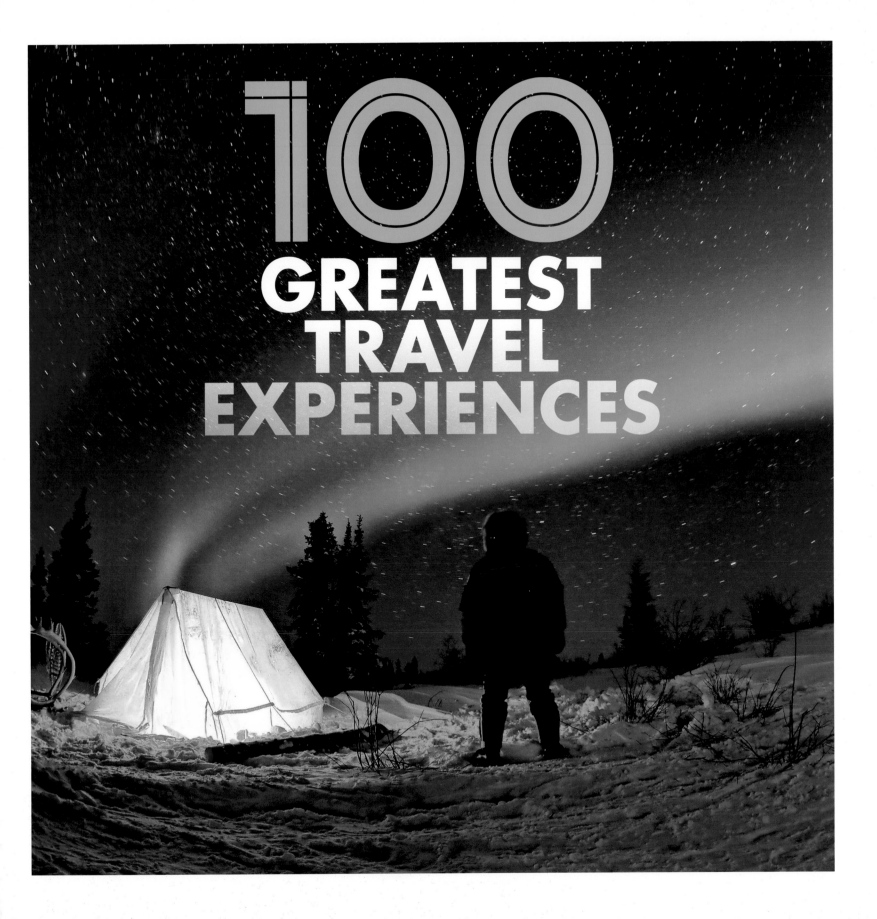

100
GREATEST
TRAVEL
EXPERIENCES

100
GREATEST
TRAVEL
EXPERIENCES

FROM THE MAKERS OF WANDERLUST MAGAZINE...

Wanderlust was launched in 1993 by Paul Morrison and Lyn Hughes. It has since become the UK's leading travel magazine, with its hallmark mix of inspirational writing and expert advice. Top-class photography has always been a feature of the magazine, aiming to show the world as it is, rather than how we might like it to be.

Published by Wanderlust Publications Ltd.
Leworth Place, Mellor Walk, Windsor, SL4 1EB, UK
Tel: +44 (0)1753 620426
Fax: +44 (0)1753 620474
Web: www.wanderlust.co.uk
Email: info@wanderlust.co.uk

Editor-in-Chief/Publisher: **Lyn Hughes**
Editor: **Phoebe Smith**
Art Director: **Graham Berridge**
Editorial: **Rhodri Andrews, Sarah Baxter, Paul Bloomfield, Nick Boulos, Tom Hawker, Mike Wright**
Operations Director: **Danny Callaghan**

There are lots of bucket-lists out there, penned by travel celebrities and publications, but where this one differs is that we asked the readers of *Wanderlust* magazine what they consider to be the world's top travel experiences, those life-defining moments that stay with us forever. We were inundated with thousands of responses. Due to the current political climate worldwide we have had to remove a couple for now, but otherwise this is the list as chosen by the keenest travellers around.

Of course, your memories of these experiences will be very personal to you. For me, #17 Milford Sound is always pouring with torrential rain, as if someone has left a tap on; #67 Sigiriya is somewhere I climbed in the heat of the midday sun, and foolishly without water, so felt terrible (but it was definitely worth it); #78 Taman Negara is a very special memory because I spent a night in a hide there and got to see a clouded leopard – a remarkable and very rare wildlife spot. But isn't creating your own experiences what travel is all about?

And if you do find yourself mentally counting how many you have done, don't fret – turn to page 144 where we have a ticklist just for you.

So, how many have you done? We love to hear from our readers about their adventurous travels, so head to www.wanderlust.co.uk to let us know where you've been. And for a regular dose of travel inspiration do check out Wanderlust magazine – for those with a passion for travel!

Happy travels,

Lyn

Lyn Hughes,
Editor-in-Chief/Publisher,
Wanderlust **Magazine**
WWW.WANDERLUST.CO.UK

100

GAZING OVER
MACHU PICCHU,
PERU

How did they do that? How did those 15th-century Inca architects construct a city of mortarless stone, on steep terraces, 2,500m up in the seemingly impenetrable Andes? Standing at the Sun Gate, catching your first glimpse of the ruins – swirled in mist and couched by vertiginous mountains – you may well ask these questions. This is engineering of the tallest order, in the most dramatic of settings – one so remote even the marauding conquistadores couldn't find it. Today, just over 100 years after explorer Hiram Bingham rediscovered the site in 1911, access is a little easier – but the views and the achievement no less impressive.

One of the most important sites of the empire, the Incas constructed this complex of 200 structures – a mix of formidable ramparts, crumbling walls and stone terraces – primarily for agriculture and religious ceremonies but it was abandoned in the 1600s after the fall of the Inca empire.

Today, it ranks at the very top of most travel bucket lists and deservedly so – if you do it right. Machu Picchu is one of South America's most notoriously overcrowded sites, so it's rarely the intimate experience that many would hope for. One way of beating the daytrippers is to book a room at the Belmond Sanctuary Lodge, located close to the iconic citadel, meaning easy morning and afternoon access... when the tour buses are thinner on the ground.

MAKE IT HAPPEN: Of course, getting to Machu Picchu – 'Old Mountain' in the native Quechua language – is half the fun. The firm favourite is the classic 43km Inca Trail: starting at Km88 (Qoriwayrachina) on the rail line out of Cusco, the hike to the ruins takes 3-4 days; permits are necessary – independent trekking is not allowed.

But that's merely one option. If you fancy something a little different, Why not horseride along the lesser-known Salkantay Trail, a journey through 15 eco-systems and high mountain passes? Feeling lazy? Non-trekkers (and riders) can catch the train from Ollantaytambo to Aguas Calientes, a 20-minute bus ride from the site.

99

HANGING OUT IN HALONG BAY, VIETNAM

The geologists will tell you it's all about tectonic friction, but we prefer the local legend: that at the request of an ancient king, a dragon spat pearls into the Gulf of Tonkin, forming a ragged barrier of 1,969 islands. Vietnam's biggest attraction has commercialised fast in recent years. It's estimated that around one million people visit each year – and for good reason.

This waterworld of ghostly limestone crags, caves and floating villages, has the eternal power to enthral.

Away from the bay, visitors can enjoy secluded picnic lunches, hike to clifftop lookouts and delve deep into cavernous caves. There's lots of opportunity to interact with the local communities, too, from the green tea sipping fishermen on floating villages to the water-based vendors who sell snacks from kayaks.

Once you've drunk in the iconic view and atmosphere of Halong Bay, you can also visit the neighbouring – and crowd-free – Bai Tu Long: the same epic seascapes but without Halong's procession of Chinese junkboats. If you want to add a less fairytale dimension to your visit, try the Vietnam War-era sites on Cat Ba island.

MAKE IT HAPPEN: Halong Bay is 180km east of Hanoi, from where budget one/two-night tours are two-a-penny; Bai Tu Long is another 30km east and could be easily added into any Halong itnerary. For a more leisurely experience, take the ferry to Cat Ba island and explore by kayak or foot.

98

TRAVELLING THE KARAKORAM HIGHWAY, PAKISTAN

The Karakoram Highway is the stuff of travel legend. It's the Silk Road, Marco Polo and the Hippy Trail all rolled into one. And it's a challenger for the greatest feat of human engineering in history – a 1,300km thoroughfare somehow carved out of and around three of the world's mightiest mountain ranges.

The route wriggles from just north of Islamabad to Kashgar in China, and there are plenty of adventures to be had along the way: averting landslides, hiking up to Fairy Meadows, avoiding collisions with rainbow-blinged trucks veering around tight bends at frightening speeds. You'll drink tea with polo players, see peaks soaring over 7,000m and spot ancient rock art by the roadside. You'll be whiplashed, butt-bruised and probably exhausted. You'll have the time of your life.

MAKE IT HAPPEN: Several tour operators offer opportunities to tackle sections – with varying degrees of length and luxury – of the Karakoram Highway.

97

SITTING ON THE SUMMIT OF STROMBOLI, ITALY

People come for the quiet and the nature, so the locals say. But they also come for 'Iddu'. Iddu is Sicillian for 'him', him being the volcano that constitutes Stromboli itself. The climb up is not a long one, about two to three hours, moving through fig trees, oleander and broom at the base to sparse shrubs further up and finally nothing but black volcanic rock. If you set off in the late afternoon, you reach the summit at dusk and are rewarded with the spectacular sight of the sun dissolving into the Tyrrhenian Sea.

The soundtrack to this is less serene, a primeval *basso profundo* that the locals refer to as '*Iddu parla*' – 'He speaks'. Hard-hat on, you spend the next hour ooh-ing and ahh-ing as fluorescent magma and vapour bubbles and hisses through the volcano's vents.

MAKE IT HAPPEN: Stromboli is a four-hour ferry or 1.5-hour hydrofoil journey from the Aeolian Island of Lipari. There is no airport.

96

SPOTTING POLAR BEARS IN
SPITSBERGEN, NORWAY

On the frozen island of Spitsbergen, almost halfway between the North Pole and the Norwegian mainland, polar bears outnumber people. Home to the northernmost settlements on earth – and some 3,000 of the furry but fearsome predators – Spitsbergen is the largest island in Svalbard, an archipelago of glaciers and meringue-like mountains. Stop-in-your-tracks scenery aside, it's also one of the best places in the world to see polar bears in the wild.

These critically endangered creatures have long been the symbol of the Arctic and most opt to see them on a cruise around Spitsbergen on an expedition vessel, where they can be sighted as they prowl the icy shores and floes on the lookout for unsuspecting seals.

There's other wildlife, too, to wow the sharp-eyed or binocular-armed. Arctic foxes, grazing reindeer (shaggy and stumpy-legged), walruses and 12 species of whale, including beluga and bowheads, also hang out here.

But the star of the show is, of course, the polar bear. And for the 2,700 permanent residents – the vast majority of whom live in the capital (and Svalbard's only 'city') Longyearbyen – existing alongside their hairy, famous neighbours is a daily challenge.

Thankfully, the bears are seldom seen around the bleak but strangely beautiful town, sat in a valley ringed by jagged mountains. Think timber cabins painted in bright colours and a hilltop cathedral where worshippers are instructed to leave their shoes and guns at the door. However, venturing beyond the town's modest remits, where skidoos replace cars across the stark valleys and endless glaciers, requires a rifle. Who knows when you may chance upon a 600kg polar bear...

A cross-country snowmobiling expedition, to ghost towns and curious mining communities is high on adventure, but for wildlife viewings the very best odds come from water-based exploration. Zodiac landings, kayaking, tundra hiking and snow-shoeing add to the drama but nothing quite compares to the unbridled thrill of spotting what you've really come to see. Thankfully, sightings of fighting males (usually squabbling over mating rights) and mothers with too-cute-for-words young cubs are not uncommon. So pack your thermals, lots of good, thick socks (because you are expected to take your shoes off when entering many shops, hotels, bars) and a spare memory card for your camera!

MAKE IT HAPPEN: Fly into Longyearbyen, and either board an expedition cruise (if you're travelling during summer), or stay on the iced-in schooner *Noorderlicht* during the long and dark months of winter. A truly memorable place to stay, this ten-cabin two-mast sailing ship was originally built in 1910 and served as part of the German navy during the Second World War. Today, it spends each summer sailing around the Arctic before mooring in Tempelfjorden, where it remains frozen in place all winter.

95 WATCHING SUNRISE AND SUNSET AT ULURU, AUSTRALIA

It's a bit like a large and lumpy sandstone canvas. Because Uluru, the outie belly button pimpling Australia's middle, is at the mercy of master painter Mother Nature; its hue shifts with the sun. Set your alarm early to see the inky Outback sky turn purple, and the sleeping monolith awaken, its nighttime shadow brightening to warm browns and rich reds with the rising sun. At midday, rays spotlight Uluru's every crag and crevice (best seen on the 10km round-rock Base Walk). Come dusk, old Ayers blazes orange – a last hurrah, before fading to black. Until tomorrow.

Many myths surround this mighty monolith. Sacred to the local Pitjantjatjara Aborigines, some believe the rock rose from the ground in grief at the death of two tribal leaders. Another more sobering legend about the rock has emerged more recently, giving a word of warning to those unable to resist the understandable temptation to take home a momento in the form of a stone, rock or handful of paprika-red sand. Hundreds of 'cursed' individuals from around the world have returned such souvenirs after experiencing bad luck and ill health. Read their stories on display in the Uluru-Kata Tjuta National Park Cultural Centre.

MAKE IT HAPPEN: The nearest airport is Ayers Rock; fly there from Sydney, Cairns, Melbourne and Alice Springs. There are various sunrise/set viewpoints within the national park: Talinguru Nyakunytjaku (meaning 'To Look From the Sanddunes') is among the best spots, a lookout that offers views of Uluru, 3km away, and Kata Tjuta (the Olgas). Find out more at www.environment.gov.au/parks/uluru.

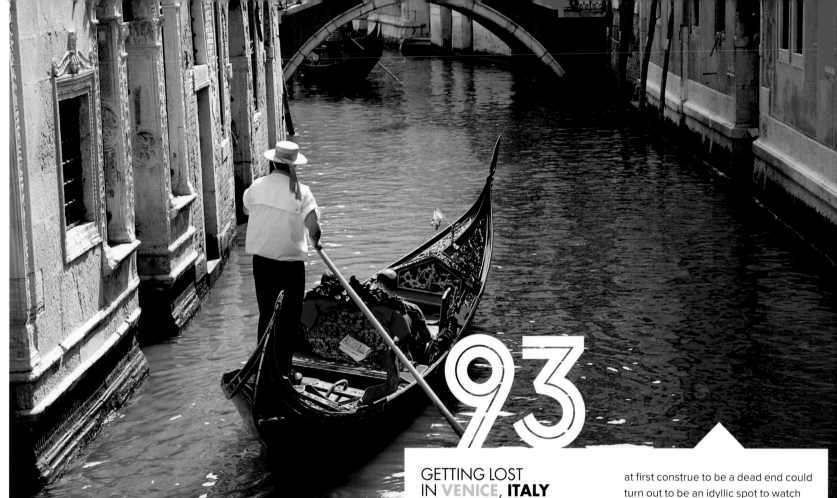

93

GETTING LOST IN VENICE, ITALY

Ah, Venice. Is there a city on earth that's easier to fall head over heels for, with its cosy corners, crumbling churches and backstreet bacari bars? However, unfortunately, this water-laced centre of romance has other suitors too... many other suitors.

But while busy Venice's most famous spots are often choked with tourists armed with selfie-sticks, it's remarkably easy to lose the masses that flood Piazza San Marco and cram onto the Rialto Bridge. How? Well, put the map down and just start walking. Because the real pleasure of Venice is not just in the sightseeing but getting well and truly lost. Away from the bustling masses outside the Doge's Palace lies a maze of courtyards, cafés and canals, quietly waiting for those who stumble upon them. Front doorsteps lead into the water, and what you might at first construe to be a dead end could turn out to be an idyllic spot to watch the gondolas float by.

When you're completely bewildered, take a water taxi out of the labyrinth and into the laguna for spectacular city panoramas, or head further out still and explore the outer islands of Murano (famed for its glasswork), Burano (its lacework) and overlooked tiny Torcello.

And if you want the main sights all to yourself, that's easy too. Visit in winter, when an eerie mist lingers over the quiet canals. It's a time when the cruise ships are nowhere to be seen and when locals reclaim their city. Take a late night stroll through Piazza San Marco and it's entirely possible that there won't be a soul, nor a selfie-stick, to be seen. Bellissimo.

MAKE IT HAPPEN: Many airlines fly to Venice's Marco Polo airport, from which you can catch a connecting bus or boat to take you into the city. High summer is best avoided.

94

UNCOVERING KYOTO, JAPAN

Kyoto really sums up what most visitors are hoping Japan would be like – full of beautiful ancient temples and traditions, with a thriving contemporary culture. The danger is not giving yourself the time it takes to not just explore the sites but also pause in the cities many quiet contemplative spots.

Visitors can do both at Kinkaku-ji, the Temple of the Golden Pavilion, one of Japan's most famous sights: gasp at the gold-covered architecture and then breathe out in beautiful gardens. Likewise, Ryoan-ji is a Zen temple with a fascinating dry-landscape rock garden.

Spend an evening wandering around Gion district, the place to see traditional teahouses, restaurants and geishas, but the best way to experience authentic Japanese hospitality – conveniently complete with delicious dishes – is to stay in a traditional *ryokan*. Get one in the heart of the city to ensure you have easy access to the many secrets this historic city has to offer, most an easy wander off the main thoroughfares.

MAKE IT HAPPEN: Fly to Tokyo; Kyoto can be reached by car, train or plane.

92

HUSKY SLEDDING IN
LAPLAND, SWEDEN

You'll hear the huskies before you ever see them. The cacophony of excited howls and barks echo around the kennels as you arrive for your sledding adventure through one of Europe's most northerly points. Because these dogs aren't pets; they are born and bred to run. And so as soon as the sledges appear in the yard and the mushers begin roping up, these canines call out, eagerly anticipating the chance for a run in the blinding white ahead of them.

Once the huskies are reined up and you're securely in the sledge, covered in layers of warm blankets and wrapped up in your specially made Arctic suit, the noise will reach a fever pitch. Then – you're off! And all the din amazingly suddenly stops.

You're plunged into the unknown of a winter's half-light and the cries of the dogs is replaced only by the rhythmic hiss as the sledge runners slice through the snow.

The chill air whisks by your face and the beauty of the Arctic wilderness begins to surround you. Weaving through the gnarled tree trunks, the bare branches seem to sparkle as the rhine-crusted bark catches the light. You'll navigate frozen lakes made as hard as a road by metres of ice and watch as clouds of powder explode into the air as you speed by.

The dogs are guided only by the occasional word from the musher or a slight tug on the reins so it comes as a surprise when you reach a clearing dotted with a cluster of

lavvu (Sami tipi-like tents) and stop. As you step off the sledge you'll be surprised to note just how deep some of the snow is, as you've spent time skirting over its surface.

At this point you might get the chance to have a go at steering your own sledge. Balancing on the runners – with your foot firmly pressed on the break – prepare to feel the speed as you signal to the huskies to move. There's nothing quite so exhilarating as guiding your own pack over the frozen tundra, leaning to the left or the right to help guide them, then battling their incredible force as you attempt to slow down.

Whether out for just a couple of hours or enjoying a few days on

the sled, the best bits comes when night falls and you settle down for a hot drink next to the glow of a log fire. The dogs are unclipped and fed and watered and finally stop and rest, quietly. Now is the time when the final piece of magic may happen. Keep a lookout towards the sky as, this far north, away from the light pollution of the big cities, if you're very lucky the aurora borealis will soon come out to play.

MAKE IT HAPPEN: Numerous tour operators offer dog-sledding trips in most Arctic regions including Sweden, Finland, Norway and Canada; you can try a single two-hour experience during your Arctic visit or head out on a full-on expedition with camping.

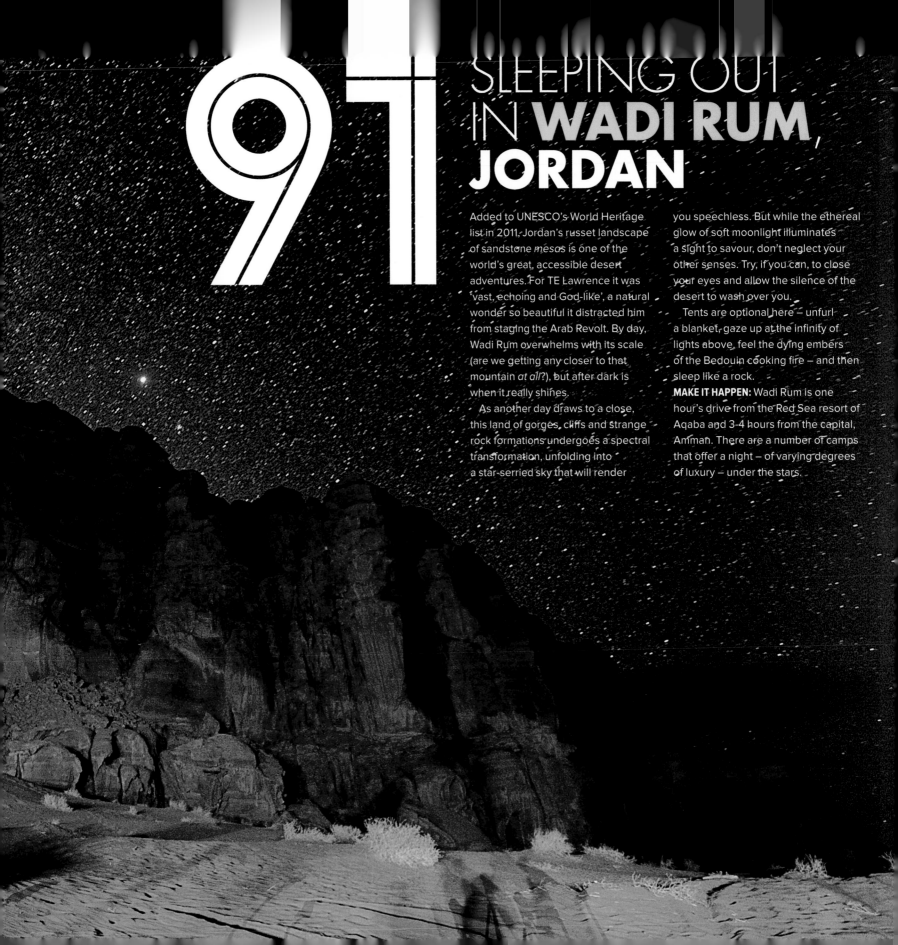

91

SLEEPING OUT IN WADI RUM, JORDAN

Added to UNESCO's World Heritage list in 2011, Jordan's russet landscape of sandstone *mesas* is one of the world's great, accessible desert adventures. For TE Lawrence it was 'vast, echoing and God-like', a natural wonder so beautiful it distracted him from staging the Arab Revolt. By day, Wadi Rum overwhelms with its scale (are we getting any closer to that mountain *at all*?), but after dark is when it really shines.

As another day draws to a close, this land of gorges, cliffs and strange rock formations undergoes a spectral transformation, unfolding into a star-serried sky that will render you speechless. But while the ethereal glow of soft moonlight illuminates a sight to savour, don't neglect your other senses. Try, if you can, to close your eyes and allow the silence of the desert to wash over you.

Tents are optional here – unfurl a blanket, gaze up at the infinity of lights above, feel the dying embers of the Bedouin cooking fire – and then sleep like a rock.

MAKE IT HAPPEN: Wadi Rum is one hour's drive from the Red Sea resort of Aqaba and 3-4 hours from the capital, Amman. There are a number of camps that offer a night – of varying degrees of luxury – under the stars.

90
OGLING IGUAÇU FALLS,
ARGENTINA/BRAZIL

"Poor Niagara" exclaimed Eleanor Roosevelt when she first set eyes on the awe-inspiring Iguaçu Falls. A fine force of nature straddling the border between Argentina and Brazil, this cataract chasm is one of the widest waterfalls in the world, consisting of 275 thunderous cascades spread in a horseshoe shape over 3km.

Start your exploration on foot, along the forested trails of Iguaçu National Park that you're likely to share with cheeky coatis (a member of the racoon family). As anticipation builds and the roar of the falls grows louder, sneak a quick peek overhead into the treetops filled with toucans and countless other tropically coloured birds. Then, prepare for a soaking.

For the most mesmerising views though, explore the upper tier tracks from the Brazilian side and descend into the mists of the 80m-high Garganta Del Diablo (Devil's Throat), where, according to legend, a demonic deity resides. It's the biggest and most impressive of all Iguaçu's falls but there are many others that deserve some attention. Stand at the foot of Floriano – named after one of Brazil's former presidents – and let the intense spray swirl around you until you're suitably drenched. It won't take long.

That spray ensures everything in these parts is well watered, leading to a profusion of green and impressive biodiversity. The subtropical forests – a mix of wild palms, Brazilian pines and tangled epiphytes and around

2,000 other plant species. The wildlife stakes are high, too. Spot pumas, somersaulting howler monkeys, anteaters and giant otters.

It's possible to get *really* close to the larger-than-life majesty with a high-octane boat ride along the coke-coloured Iguazu River, where rainbows rise from the craggy gorges. Prepare for a white knuckle ride and prepare to get wet. Again.

No other waterfall on Earth comes close. Poor Niagara indeed.

MAKE IT HAPPEN: Puerto Iguazú, Argentina, is a 90-minute flight from Buenos Aires. Buses run to the visitor centre; from here, walk or take a quick train ride to the falls. Foz do Iguaçu, Brazil, is a 90-min flight from São Paulo; the falls are a short drive from there.

89

SEE A CONTINENT BY
INTERRAILING, EUROPE

How many travelling lives have started with a scrimped-and-saved-for InterRail ticket and a copy of the *Thomas Cook European Rail Timetable*? Since 1973, the hop-on-hop-off continental rail pass has been a rite of passage for Europeans, the budget Grand Tour – and every InterRailer has their tale to tell. Breathtaking trundles through the Swiss Alps. Sardine-like squeezes through old Yugoslavia. Sleeping on deck on the Patras-Brindisi ferry. Border snarl-ups, sleep deprivation, hospitable strangers, romantic adventures and everything in between: the only certainty is that, after a month, your free ride is up.

The sense of adventure may remain the same but some things *have* changed since those heady days of the Seventies. A new app makes planning this cross-continent adventure easier than ever before and there's greater choice in destinations and accommodation. What are you waiting for?

MAKE IT HAPPEN: InterRail passes are now available for all ages and various durations: see www.interrailnet.com.

88

JOURNEYING TO THE
JOKHANG & POTALA
PALACE, LHASA, TIBET

Sitting high on the top of Red Mountain at the end of the long Lhasa Valley, the Potala Palace has been one of the more arresting sights in the world since the 7th century. A quiet, solemn place, with tall stonewalls and a thousand rooms, it acts as a poignant reminder that something fundamental has been missing from Tibetan life since the Dalai Lama fled in 1959. Before then, though, the splendid palace, served as one of the official residences of the iconic figure.

Elsewhere, Jokhang Temple, in the centre of old Lhasa, is proof that the nation's spiritual life still goes on. It's a kaleidoscope of colourful prayer flags and trinket stalls where monks and farmers jostle for position on the pilgrim path that surrounds it. At its heart sits a temple where each morning crimson-robed monks chant in the glower of a thousand yak-butter candles. It's a place that moves all those who journey to this troubled enclave nestled deep among sacred mountain peaks.

But spiritual and altitudinal highs are scattered all over Tibet. Pilgrims flock to Lake Manasarovar, revered by Tibetans, not just to stand beside one of the planet's highest lakes but to bathe in its waters and walk the 90km around its shores, a journey of 4-5 days. But you don't have to follow in their footsteps to realise that Tibet is the most life-affirming of destinations.

MAKE IT HAPPEN: Trains run from Xining to Lhasa; journey time is around 24 hours. Overland tours run from Nepal.

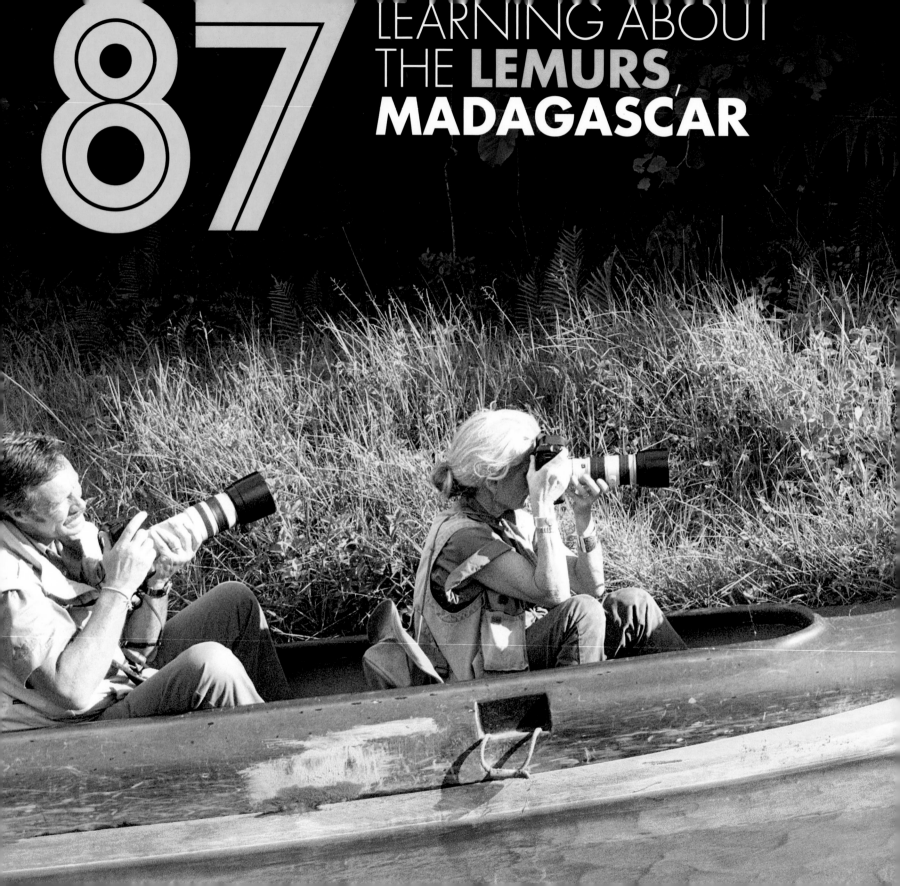

Madagascar is the oldest island on earth, and its flora and fauna have evolved in isolation over tens of millions of years. It split from Gondwanaland before big predators had developed and, instead of chimps or gorillas, Madagascar developed lemurs, a gentle, unaggressive, cheeky and inquisitive primate. There are 86 different species recognised, ranging from mouse lemurs (the smallest primate in the world) up to the indri, the size of a chimpanzee, with an amazing call that can be heard up to 1km away.

The call of the wild is what waits on this vast island – the fourth largest on earth (roughly the size of France). It's a land of spiny deserts, tropical rainforests, golden beaches and coral reef, and forests infused with the scent of vanilla – one of the country's biggest exports. Together, they form rare and complex eco-systems that shelter all manner of weird and wonderful creatures. There's hard-to-spot chameleons and Madagascar's largest predator: the cat-like fossa.

Of course, the real stars of the show are the lemurs. Incredibly there were once lemurs the size of gorillas, but sadly they are now extinct. The species that are still alive and kicking are found in different locations across the country. Ring-tail lemurs – the poster boy of Madagascan wildlife – favour the south while the equally-adorable indri lemurs can be seen (and heard) in Andasibe-Mantadia National Park to the east.

Tree-swinging primates aside, the flora of Madagascar is no less impressive with a staggering 12,000 species. All in all, a stunning 80% of it is endemic, found nowhere else on the planet. Like the world's ultimate garden centre, botanist enthusiasts can tick off the 1,000 types of orchid and walk along wide avenues lined with bulbous baobab trees. According to legend, these 'upside down' trees were created by an infuriated God who ripped them from the ground and replanted them the other way round to stop them from walking off...

MAKE IT HAPPEN: Fly to capital Antananarivo (known as Tana), via France, Kenya or South Africa. April/May and October/November are the best times to visit.

86

PLUNGING INTO THE WILDERNESS, ALASKA, USA

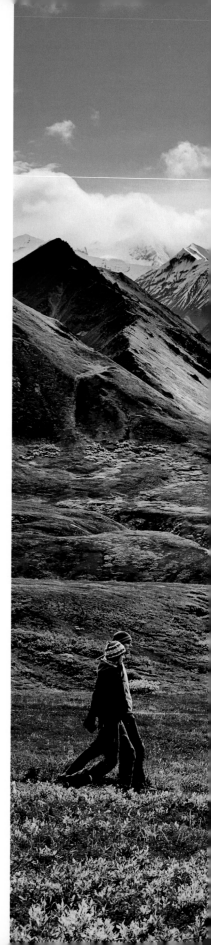

North America is renowned for dishing up huge portions, but it's outdone itself with Alaska. The Last Frontier State is the USA's biggest – but its least densely populated. It has 17 of the country's 20 tallest mountains, topping out at the formidable 6,194m Mt McKinley, which also happens to be the highest point on the continent. Described by experts as a harder mountain to summit than Everest due partly to the harsh Arctic conditions, it was first scaled in 1913 by a team of four led by British priest, Hudson Stuck.

Back down at ground level, there's 70,000km of coastline, 300 rivers and around 100,000 glaciers. Put simply, it does wilderness on a gargantuan scale. As a consequence, you can get wonderfully lost almost anywhere. Try

Denali National Park if you've got a head for heights, the Aleutian island chain if you prefer the sea, or the Arctic-tickling Dalton Highway for a very different kind of American roadtrip.

The latter is a drive that not only showcases epic Arctic scenery but also some of Alaska's strangest settlements. The curious trucker town of Coldfoot is one of the few communities found north of the Arctic Circle. With a permanent population of just ten, not a great deal goes on but it's an intriguing place frequented by long distance lorry drivers with a wealth of stories to share. A few miles up the road is Wiseman, which boasts a swelling population of 14. Don't miss peeking inside the abandoned log-built Post Office that's been sinking into the ground for the past century.

For many, though, bear watching is the real name of the game. And there's nowhere better than Katmai National Park. Located 400km southwest of Anchorage, this wilderness – encompassing volcanoes, glaciers, meadows and lakes – is stalked by 2,200 brown bears.

The money shot for bear spotters happens along the fast-flowing Brook River, where peckish bears congregate to feast on the salmon travelling from the Bering Sea. The best times to catch the spectacle is July and September.

MAKE IT HAPPEN: May-August is the best time to visit; winters are long and cold, and snow can make some areas inaccessible. For more information, head to www.travelalaska.com

85

GETTING SPIRITUAL ON THE GANGES, INDIA

Mata Ganga, or 'Mother Ganges', is central to India's sense of itself, a formidable river that's also the spiritual backbone of the subcontinent. From its source high in the Himalayas, the river cuts diagonally west to east, emptying out into the Bay of Bengal 2,510km later. Along its route lie some of India's most sacred cities – Haridwar, Varanasi and Allahabad among them. Head north to Haridwar (and its similarly venerable neighbour, Rishikesh) and experience the Ganges at its freshest (and cleanest).

It's here, too, that you'll witness the moving *aarti* ceremony at dusk, where candles set in tiny boats made from flowers (known as *diyas*), float in their thousands down the river, carrying with them the hopes of millions of believers.

MAKE IT HAPPEN: Fly direct to Delhi. From here, take a train to Haridwar and use buses or taxis to visit nearby Rishikesh. For more information go to www.incredibleindia.org.

84

MEET THE LOCALS IN ISFAHAN, IRAN

The warmth of the Iranian people is legendary but, in truth, it's more scorching than warm. Anyone out for an early evening's stroll through Isfahan's grand Imam Square – the minarets of the Shah Mosque standing tall against the setting sun, the last rays of the day bouncing off its blue glazed tiles – can discover what it's like to be a celebrity as the delighted locals gather around, armed with their camera phones, Cheshire-cat grins and a million and one questions. 'Do you like Iran? Is it how you imagined? Are the people treating you well?'

Between offers of tea and requests for your phone number, visitors can spot the horses speeding around the square like cars on a racetrack. They pull carts laden with Iranian families, likely to wave and squeal with delight as they see you. Even the local picnicking women, cloaked in jet black chadors, sat on the grass nearby, won't be too busy to smile as you pass by. Heartwarming indeed.

MAKE IT HAPPEN: Fly to Tehran; Isfahan is 400km to the south.

83

HIKING THE TONGARIRO CROSSING, NEW ZEALAND

It's touted as New Zealand's – if not the world's – best day walk. Quite a claim. But this 19km tramp across the volcanically sculpted wilds of North Island is a contender. It's a manageable challenge, for starters – at six-to eight hours it will test but not break you. Then there's the variety: from the shrubby Mangatepopo Valley, to the lunar weirdness of Red Crater, the sulphurous sparkles of Blue and Emerald Lakes and, finally, the descent into lush podocarp forest.

Throw in some bubbling hot springs and craters spewing sulphurous steam and you've got quite the adventure. Add some Maori legend, and a sprinkle of Hollywood glam (Tongariro starred in *The Lord of the Rings* trilogy, posing as Mordor, home of the evil Lord Sauron), and world-class status is in the bag.

Keen for even more? Consider the three-hour round-trip to the top of Mount Ngauruhoe – Mount Doom itself – from the South Crater. It's a steep, fairly strenuous ascent to the 2,287m summit but the strange landscapes of old lava flows and rocky ridges are more than enough to keep you entertained. And the views? Expect larger-than-life panoramas of Mount Taranaki to the west, the snow-capped Kaimanawa Range and, on a clear day, Lake Taupo.

MAKE IT HAPPEN: The Crossing starts from Mangatepopo Road end, 6km off Highway 47; it finishes at Ketetahi Roadend. Local operators can arrange transfers. www.doc.govt.nz

82
DELVING INTO THE DUNES OF
SOSSUSVLEI, **NAMIBIA**

There are sand dunes, and there are *sand dunes*. And the Namib Desert's offerings in this arena are the Himalaya of the granular world: the dunes here tower up to 300m, massive undulations that shape-shift with the wind. They're not just big, they're beautiful – gracefully curved, rippled as the sea and apricot-orange under a perennial blue sky.

There are many ways to experience the Sossusvlei area and choosing how to is very much a personal decision. Many opt for a thrilling (and heart-thumping) ascent of the elegant S-sweep of Dune 45, named so because it's located 45km from the small settlement of Sesriem. It's particularly popular – and wildly spectacular – at sunrise. From the top, you can take in the widescreen vastness of the valley, punctuated with countless dunes that rise and fall like billowing sails. Standing chief among them is the aptly-named Big Daddy, the tallest of Sossusvlei's dunes at 325m. Some choose to take in the splendour from an even greater height by lifting off in a hot air balloon for the ultimate overview.

But Sossusvlei is more than just a collection of dramatic dunes. Hike to the dramatic tree-trunk graveyard of Dead Vlei, an eerie bleached-white clay pan peppered with the remains of craggy camel thorn trees thought to be around 700 years old but have escaped from decomposing due to the dry climate.

But life thrives here despite the harsh conditions of this most inhospitable of lands. Some, like the emblematic oryx, which appears on the Namibian coat of arms, are easily spotted but other creatures are harder to come across. Take, for example, the translucent palmato gecko, which resides deep in the sand to survive in the inhospitable climate only to emerge at night to feed. With no eyelids, they keep their big eyes clean by licking them. If you really want to get under the skin (and sand) of Sossusvlei, a 'desert discovery' tour with a local naturalist guide, trained in reading the ripples of the dunes for tell-tell signs of lurking lizards, will help reveal all manner of secrets.

MAKE IT HAPPEN: Fly to the capital, Windhoek. Sossusvlei is 590km to the west. It's accessible by 2WD; a 4WD is necessary for the final 5km to Sossusvlei Pan (or walk from the car park).

81
BROWSING HOI AN,
VIETNAM

You come for the culture, but you'll stay for the clothes. Vietnam's most atmospheric traveller town is an elegant waterfront harbour of 18th-century merchant houses adorned with lanterns, ornate pagodas and French colonial airs. You'll nose into museums, sip *café au laits* overlooking the Thu Bon River – and then you'll buy clothes.

Whimsical suits for £20 (why not?), shimmery cocktail dresses, a couple of shirts, one like that from *GQ* or *Vogue* (the magazines well-leafed) – and before you know it, you have fitting appointments all over town, and a spiralling set of bills. Shop carefully and you'll still be wearing well-made mementoes from Hoi An a decade later.

While the town's tailors are hard at work sewing, stitching and seaming,

you'll have plenty of time to explore Hoi An's many cultural highlights. Start at Tan Ky House, a beautiful heritage property (just one of the 1,107 in the town). It's been in the same family for generations since it was built two centuries ago and its oldy-worldy facade, a mix of Japanese and Chinese touches, is the first hint of the architectural brilliance that awaits inside.

Once used to receive old merchants, the interior is one of wooden balconies, courtyards and columns. Mosaics and old Chinese poems, expertly carved in mother of pearl, decorate the walls. It's a pint-sized pad, with just four rooms packed with dusty antiques but remains one of Hoi An's most charming addresses.

Travellers fall for Hoi An hook, line and sinker, and the Vietnamese government are determined to keep it that way. They've declared that shopkeepers are required by law to hang paper lanterns from their properties.

But shopping is the name of the game in Hoi An, and it's not all fashion focused either. The riverside Central Market – one of Vietnam's most colourful – is an exhilarating centre of commerce with spices, silk, chuckling chickens and fresh fish exchanging hands. Visit at around 6am to see the fishermen bring in the catch of the day.
MAKE IT HAPPEN: Hoi An is halfway between Saigon and Hanoi; the nearest train station is 30km away at Danang. Remember to leave space in your bags for a new wardrobe.

80

WATERHOLE-WATCHING IN ETOSHA NATIONAL PARK, NAMIBIA

Namibia is vast – yet, at times, it seems as if nobody else is there. Combining sweeping desert, deep canyons, 1,572km of coastline and a tiny population, it feels truly wild. Consequently, you might not see many people, but then you will see wildlife – seemingly without even trying to. Head to the world's biggest sand dunes and you'll spy long-horned oryx amid the silt, drive along the network of wonderfully empty roads and be accompanied by springbok sprinting alongside you and even heading into town you'll often spot baboons hanging out on the kerb.

Namibia is also a spectacular conservation success story – it has the world's largest population of cheetahs, the largest population of black rhinos, and growing numbers of lions. To experience all of them in one spot head to the famed pans of Etosha National Park.

Once there you can self-drive around waterholes where the wildlife gather. Water is a scarce commodity in this dry calcrete pan of Etosha. Not great news for the animals but good for those who want to watch them. With so few puddles in the park, particularly during the dry season, it's ready made for viewing.

The best time to head there is in the evening. It's a waiting game but eventually, your patience will pay off as, one-by-one, animals of all shapes and sizes will begin to stop by for a drink. From lions to giraffes, zebras and elephants and – hopefully – one of their black rhinos.

MAKE IT HAPPEN: Etosha is a six-hour drive north of Windhoek. Three government camps within the park have floodlit waterholes for nighttime wildlife-viewing.

79

WATCHING WHALES IN THE GULF OF ST LAWRENCE, CANADA

Despite a history of whalers firing their harpoons here, the deep and krill-filled St Lawrence River remains one of the world's greatest whalewatching waterways. Thirteen species of large mammals have been spotted in its leviathan flow, which slices Québec from south of Montréal to the gaping Gulf of St Lawrence – the spot where three currents collide, stimulating plankton development and providing a veritable feast for the waiting cetaceans.

Come here to see acrobatic humpbacks, 25m-long blues, almost-as-massive fins and seemingly smiling belugas. There's so much marine action – also keep an eye out for seal, porpoise, dolphin and snow goose – you can often see it from land, but best is to hop in a zodiac or kayak and paddle out into the whales' world.

MAKE IT HAPPEN: Peak season is May-September. Boat trips leave from spots such as Tadoussac and Baie-Sainte-Catherine. Spot from land on the 900km Whale Route along the North Shore.

78

HIKING TAMAN NEGARA NATIONAL PARK, MALAYSIA

At 130 million years old, the Taman Negara rainforest deserves a little respect when you step under her hallowed canopy. Lying 150km north-east of Kuala Lumpur, this awesome 4,000 sq km jungle is home to herds of elephants, *Orang Asli* hunter-gatherers and mysterious caves and rivers.

The Gua Telinga caves are a tight squeeze and surprisingly deep, yet whip spiders and thousands of tiny roundleaf fruitbats all survive in their cavernous depths. Elsewhere, canopy walkways are slung between strong trees, where gibbons and hill squirrels slouch in the branches. Longer hikes, such as the seven-dayer to the Four Steps waterfall, offer full-on jungle immersion.

MAKE IT HAPPEN: Kuala Tahan is the gateway town – get there from Kuala Lumpur by train or bus via Jerantut. Tours can be booked locally or in Kuala Lumpur.

77

DIVING THE
GREAT BARRIER REEF, AUSTRALIA

Bigger isn't always better. But sometimes it is – witness the Great Barrier Reef, some 2,300km of coral fringing the east coast of Australia, comprising nearly 3,000 separate reefs and 900 islands: in short, it's the largest living structure in the world. It's so huge that it's visible from space – but it is most thrilling viewed up close, on a scuba dive.

Though the coral itself can be gorgeous, it's the spectacular marine life living among, above and around the reef that you're really here to see. Some 1,625 fish species share the water with thousands of species of mollusc, starfish, turtles, sea snakes, whales and dolphins.

Different stretches of reef offer different attractions: coral is closest to the shore near Cairns, while from Airlie Beach you can combine diving with a visit to the paradisiacal beaches of the Whitsunday Islands. At the reef's far southern tip, Lady Elliot Island is the place to swim with huge manta rays, but you can encounter sharks – mostly black-tip or white-tip reef shark or the sofa-like wobbegong – on any dive. And sweat the small stuff: some of the most beautiful creatures are tiny nudibranches and crustaceans.

In short: dive shallow or deep, close to shore or on remote outer reaches, north or south, day or night – just get under the surface and explore.

MAKE IT HAPPEN: Key hubs for reef diving trips include Port Douglas and Cairns in the north, and Airlie Beach for the Whitsunday Islands further south.

76

MARVELLING AT THE
MAYAN RUINS OF TIKAL,
GUATEMALA

At the same time as Rome was founded, a mighty empire was burgeoning in Central America – one that lasted much, much longer, yet is still shrouded in mystery. At its peak, the land of the Maya stretched from the tip of the Yucatán Peninsula in the north to the Pacific coast of Guatemala in the south, and from the lush jungles of what's now Mexico's Chiapas state in the west to the caye-fringed Caribbean shores of Belize. Its pyramidal temples loom over the cliffs of Tulum, soar from the rainforest at Palenque, draw the crowds at Chichén Itzá and lie largely hidden in the dense greenery at El Mirador in remote northern Guatemala.

Most striking of all, though, are the temples of Tikal in north-eastern Guatemala. Buried in the jungle,

shrouded in mist and serenaded by macaws and howler monkeys, the site was first settled by the Maya around 900 BC. Over the centuries it grew in power and size, reaching a peak in the eighth century AD, when it was the greatest city in the Maya world, home to perhaps 100,000 people.

Within a century it had fallen into a decline – still unexplained – and its distinct pyramid-shaped towers were abandoned to the jungle. Cloaked by the thick foliage, the ruins were missed by Hernán Cortés as he marched his conquistador troops past in 1525, and was only reintroduced to the wider world by the sketches of artist Eusebio Lara in 1848. Yet its wonders merely slumbered, waiting to be explored: thousands of buildings remain in the

16 sq km core of the ancient city, deep in the tangled interior of the Petén Basin, and only half a dozen of the main temples have so far been excavated and restored.

The iconic Temple of the Grand Jaguar and Temple of the Masks guard the central Great Plaza – climb the latter temple to watch the sun set over the primordial jungle from a 38m-high vantage point, or head to 65m Temple IV for even more dramatic vistas from the highest structure in pre-Columbian America.

But there's much more to explore here: wander among the carved stone stelae standing to attention in the Great Plaza, or delve into the jungle to play Indiana Jones – it's estimated that perhaps 30% of the temples and other

structures at Tikal are yet to be unearthed. You're bound to enjoy wild encounters en route, passing trails of leaf-cutter ants, spotting a toucan perched in a branch, or disturbing a gaggle of wild turkeys – some 285 bird species have been recorded here.

Just don't leave your bag unattended: the local coatis, raccoon-type creatures, have light paws and a penchant for muesli bars.

MAKE IT HAPPEN: Flores is the gateway town for Tikal, served by flights from Guatemala City. The minibus ride from Flores to Tikal takes around 75 minutes. Tikal is open 6am-6pm, but most tour buses arrive late morning and leave by mid-afternoon; stay overnight to catch sunset and sunrise at the site, and enjoy the atmosphere in peace.

74

BOATING ALONG
THE MEKONG, **LAOS**

Rising in the mountains of China's Yunnan province, the Mekong River flows over 4,000km through Burma, Laos, Thailand and Cambodia before fanning out into its lush delta in Vietnam. In most of these countries the Mekong is more than just a river: it's the aorta of South-East Asia, a highway, a larder, a border, a playground.

A voyage along the Mekong is the quintessential experience for travellers in Laos – one in which the destination is less important than the journey. The most popular route meanders downstream from the Thai border at Huay Xai to Luang Prabang, that laidback town of gilt-roofed temples and French colonial villas perched on the hillside overlooking the confluence of the Mekong and Nam Khan rivers.

If getting to Luang Prabang is the main objective, you could leap aboard a narrow (and none-too-safe) speedboat and make the journey in a few short, uncomfortable hours. If money's no object, luxurious boats dawdle on a two- or three-day cruise along the same stretch. But for most, the two-day slow boat provides the time to enjoy the views of karst mountains and rice fields, fishing boats hauling in a catch and children splashing in the shallows.

The languid pace also allows for calls at traditional villages, an overnight at the pit-stop town of Pakbeng and a pause to gawp at the caves at Pak Ou, packed with thousands of small Buddha images, 25km upstream from Luang Prabang. Mostly, though, the voyage is a chance to let your thoughts drift with the current and soak up life on the river.

MAKE IT HAPPEN: Slow boats depart daily for Luang Prabang from the Thai border at Huay Xai – you can overnight at Pakbeng. You can also take the boat upstream from Luang Prabang, which makes for a slightly slower (but less busy) journey to Huay Xai.

75

ADMIRING
YELLOWSTONE
NATIONAL PARK,
WYOMING, USA

If you thought Iceland was, volcanically speaking, where it's at, think again. Take a trip into the heart of the Rocky Mountains and you'll find a wilderness ruled by extremes of fire and ice. Fed by the energy of a volcanic caldera, half of the whole world's geothermal features – some 10,000 sites – are located in Yellowstone. They include burbling mudpots, sulphurous cauldrons and the explosive Old Faithful geyser.

Oh, and there's wildlife galore too: American icons such as grizzly bears, elk, bison and wolves. You can drive the figure-of-eight-shaped road system to visit the best-known sights, but this is a place to revel in the Great Outdoors. Hike the Fairy Falls trail and wonder at the Grand Prismatic Spring. Join a ranger-led nature walk, or try rafting through the rapids and scenery of Beartrap Canyon.

MAKE IT HAPPEN: From the nearest international airport at Salt Lake City, Yellowstone is a 625km drive. Domestic flights to Jackson or Cody in Wyoming will take you within 80km of the park.

73

HOVERING OVER FRANZ JOSEF GLACIER, NEW ZEALAND

Remote, rugged and absolutely remarkable, New Zealand alone is top of many travellers' wishlists. If it wowed you on the big screen in films such as *The Lord of the Rings*, New Zealand will knock you with the force of an All Blacks prop forward when you actually take the time to visit it.

With its high peaks, volcanic grumbling, weird wildlife, raging waters and high-octane thrills, it is the ultimate outdoor playground – and it can be hard pressed to choose the best experience on offer as there are so many.

The two main islands – North and South – have different characters. North Island is warmer, with more rolling hills, beautiful beaches and some seriously sulphurous volcanic goings-on: such as Rotorua for the best thermal bath or Tongariro National Park to see still-active craters in an otherworldly landscape.

But then there's the dramatic South Island – which has the highest peaks, glacier-carved fiords – a trip to Fiordland will show Mother Nature at her most artistic. And then there are the actual glaciers themselves.

With more than 60 giant sheets of ice sliding down to the west coast of New Zealand's south, this is the ultimate place to get up close and personal with the creaking white tongues, as old as the hills themselves.

Franz Josef is one of the most impressive you'll find, galloping from the 3,000m highs of the Southern Alps to sea level in just a few kilometres. The result: glacial drama on a grand scale.

Perhaps the coolest way to appreciate its scale and raw beauty is from above. Swoop over in a helicopter and you'll be able to get a bird's eye view of all the ice-action in detail. From the comfort of your seat (though you'll likely be on the edge of it) enjoy the feeling of hovering in the air while effortlessly looking down on chilling crevasses, towering seracs and sculpted caves.

The more intrepid-minded can take it further still by getting your experienced pilot to land on the snowfields too. From there, geared up in warm layers, you can experience the thrill of actually walking on this slowly shifting geological monster.

Feel the chill of the cool air whip into your face as you navigate the ice tunnels surrounded in corridors of turquoise. It will feel very much as if you've left the earth behind as you slip and slide your way between the layers and squeeze under frozen curtains of dripping icicles, watch your guide carve and hack steps into the frozen terrain and teeter your way over ladders lain horizontal for you to traverse the gaps. Chilling and thrilling in equal measure.

MAKE IT HAPPEN: Several operators offer helicopter trips over Fox and Franz Josef glaciers; scenic flights last 20-40 minutes (with snow landing), heli-hiking tours last three hours. There's also the option to explore the glaciers on foot – most companies include the hire of technical gear, such as crampons, ice axes and boots, as well as qualified guides.
For more: www.glaciercountry.co.nz.

72
FLYING OVER THE
SKELETON COAST,
NAMIBIA

A ghoulish name for an eerie area: north-west Namibia's Skeleton Coast is a no-man's land of starkly spectacular proportions. It's a place where bleached whale bones and the rusting hulks of shipwrecks line miles of empty sand; where shores sparkle with gem stones; where a few resilient animals – jackal, oryx, desert-adapted elephant – patrol the dunes.

Skeleton Coast National Park stretches north for 500km up to the border with Angola, and it's best to witness this vastness from above: up here you can see in widescreen the battle of land and sea, which the relentless Atlantic appears to be winning.

MAKE IT HAPPEN: The 200km from Swakopmund to the Ugab River is the National West Coast Tourist Recreational Area; no permits are required. Skeleton Coast National Park begins at the Ugab; the far north, between the Hoanib and Kunene rivers, can only be visited by fly-in tour. www.skeletoncoastsafaris.com.

71
KAYAKING IN FIORDLAND, SOUTH ISLAND, NEW ZEALAND

Water is not in short supply in Fiordland National Park. This glacially gouged chunk of South Island's south-west is riven with inlets, well rinsed by waterfalls, and receives a sou'wester-splattering 8m of rain each year. So, unsurprisingly, taking to the water is the best way to see it. More well-known is Milford Sound, but even more remote than that is Doubtful Sound, the name given by James Cook, who harboured concerns about whether he would be able to take his ship through it or not.

You won't need to be concerned with a similar issue if you take a much more manoeuvrable kayak — the ideal vessel for paddling into quiet coves and bays unreachable on foot, and for getting a sea-level introduction to the fur seals, penguins and bottlenose dolphins that call it home.

MAKE IT HAPPEN: Te Anau is Fiordland's main hub. From there it's a 20km drive to Manapouri, followed by a 30km boat trip across the lake to reach Doubtful Sound.

70
TAKING TO TWO-WHEELS BIKING, VIETNAM

You don't have to be crazy to want to cycle or motorcycle in Vietnam, but it helps. Ho Chi Minh City is a maelstrom of scooters, cycles and cyclos. If you see a break in the traffic, go for it. Just make sure that the guy with a dozen live ducks hanging off his handlebars doesn't beat you to it.

Thankfully things get a little more zen outside of the cities. Here you'll find timeless Vietnam. Watercolour mountains; conical-hatted workers bobbing among the rice paddies; a toothless old man herding ducks along the road; a girl cycling by in a blindingly white *ao dai* tunic uttering a shy 'hello Mister' (or Mrs). Magic.

Head north along the winding mountain roads to the misty terraced hillsides of Sapa, home to hilltribes and some of South-East Asia's best scenery. Then come back down to sea level gradually, progressing south down the spine of the country via its handsome capital, rice fields, coastal resorts and colonial towns.

Visit old imperial palaces and stop at roadside stalls and slurp down a steaming bowl of *pho* (noodle soup traditionally served with beef or chicken). It promises to be the ride of your life.

MAKE IT HAPPEN: The best time to visit Vietnam is November-April, the dry season — though the highlands can be chilly at this time. Fly to Hanoi or Ho Chi Minh City (Saigon) to gain access to the country then hire your wheels. It's worth getting a guide to show you the road rules.

69

ROAMING ROME & THE VATICAN, ITALY

If Rome was a gelato (a food, incidentally, in which the city excels) it would be tutti frutti – a speckled confection of countless fruits and flavours. Because in the Italian capital the remnants of 2,000 years of habitation are scattered liberally: an ancient column supports a modern house; a motorway follows the curve of a millennia-old road. It's a metropolis-sized museum, endlessly intriguing.

The big sites are obvious: Colosseum, Forum, the Vatican... But it's the cumulation of so much old in one place that makes Rome so delicious. Built on the banks of the Tiber River, this city has been at the very epicentre of humanity for centuries.

So, where to begin? The Colosseum – the ancient amphitheatre, site of bloody gladiatorial battles and now Rome's most iconic sight – is the obvious starting point. But don't waste hours queuing for admission. Instead, stroll across the road to the crowd-free desk at the Roman Forum – another unmissable element to any trip to the Italian capital – and buy a ticket there. Not only will it allow access to the impressive ruins, built in part by Julius Caesar, but also grants fast-track entry to the Colosseum.

From there, climb the Spanish Steps, stand under the oculus of the 2nd century Pantheon, marvel at the marbled masterpiece of Il Vittoriano, built to commemorate the country's first king.

Then tick off as many of the city's 1,000 churches as you can. But if you only make it to one then it really ought to be the gilded glory of St Peter's Basilica in the Vatican, the focal point for one billion Catholics all over the world. The walled sovereign state was granted independence by Mussolini in 1929 and mints its own euros and even has its own postage stamps.

Want to catch sight of the Pope himself? The Pontiff gives a free blessing most Wednesdays. Tickets can be collected from the Swiss Guards at the Bronze Doors on the day.

An audience with His Holiness aside, it would be sacrilege to visit and not gaze up at Michelangelo's masterpiece on the ceiling of the Sistine Chapel. Part of the Vatican Museums, entry costs €16 but is free on the last Sunday of each month. Arrive early to avoid a lengthy wait.

Then eat, eat and eat some more. The pasta at Hostaria da Pietro is heavenly and the pizza at Il Corallo (try all 23 varieties) is poetry on plate. Finish off your Italian feast with a scoop of gelato from Gelateria del Teatro, masterminded by Stefano Marcotulli, the Willy Wonka of ice-cream. Think white chocolate with basil. It's nicer than it sounds.

Whatever you do, don't leave Rome without throwing a penny into the ornate Trevi Fountain to ensure your return to the Eternal City. Or so the tradition goes...

MAKE IT HAPPEN: Fly to Rome's Fiumicino airport and take the shuttle bus or the train to the centre. The city is best avoided in the summer when it's excessively hot and crowded.

68 MEETING MOUNTAIN GORILLAS, RWANDA & UGANDA

Ask anyone who has made eye contact with a gorilla, and they'll tell you it's the experience of a lifetime. With only around 700-800 of them left (they are listed as 'Critically Endangered') it certainly is a rare and privileged treat. In the years since David Attenborough sat surrounded by gorillas in the BBC's *Life on Earth*, the mountain gorilla has become something of an icon for ecotourism and conservation. To see them you need to head to a the Virunga Conservation Area (includes parts of Rwanda, the Democratic Republic of Congo and Uganda).

A guide will lead you to them, but it can take hours of trekking in the hot and humid forest, with the ever growing worry that you won't see one. But when you finally do, when that giant hominid looks you in the face, that will be a moment that will stay with you forever.

MAKE IT HAPPEN: For Rwanda, fly to Kigali. For Uganda, fly to Entebbe, near Kampala. In Rwanda, gorilla-trekking permits cost US$750; Uganda is US$600, though off-season permits are less: see www.ugandawildlife.org

67

STANDING ATOP THE ROCK CITY OF SIGIRIYA, SRI LANKA

You can't exactly miss Sigiriya. This monumental magma plug soars up 180m from the surrounding greenery of central Sri Lanka, dominating the jungly scene. Which probably explains why King Kashyapa I – who ruled from AD 477 to 495 – decided to build a palace and fortress complex on its top: it's too good a spot not to use. Building here was an incredible feat of human ingenuity. Somehow, those fifth-century masons and labourers managed to construct pleasure gardens and palaces on and around this monolith – plenty of traces of which still exist today.

At Sigiriya's entrance, beyond the double moat, lie the Water Gardens, where you can imagine the former grandeur of the pools, pavilions and fountains; the latter, which work using pressure and gravity, still spurt water after heavy rains, despite being 1,500 years old. Beyond this sits the Boulder Gardens of the lower palace, where King Kashyapa would no doubt have lolled and strolled; there are also older monastic remains here – inscriptions in some of the caves suggest they were used by monks between the third century BC and the first century AD.

It's a climb of 1,200 steps to reach the top of the behemothic boulder. First, the stairs lead up to the Terrace Garden, from where spiral staircases – a nineteenth-century addition – swirl up to the Sigiriya Damsels. A cave in the rock-side is daubed with around 20 lovely ladies (though it's believed there were originally 500). They are possibly representations of celestial nymphs, and they are certainly beguiling; look out for the one with an extra nipple.

After the damsels comes a narrow, cliff-clinging walkway that runs alongside the Mirror Wall. This was once a strip of high-sheen beeswax, egg-white and lime plaster – allegedly so thoroughly polished that the king could see his reflection in it; now it is less lustrous and scribbled with graffiti, some of which dates back to the seventh century.

Nearly there now. After the Mirror Wall you reach the giant stone claws of the Lion's Gate. The paws are all that remain of the enormous feline statue that once guarded the entrance to Sigiriya's inner sanctum; those permitted access would have had to walk through the lion's gaping mouth.

Sadly, little of King Kashyapa's rock-top eyrie has survived, though foundations can still be seen, spreading across the spacious summit plateau and indicating the incredible scale of the place. There are the remains of terraces and gardens, plus a large water tank thought to have been fed from below by a clever system of hydraulics.

But the main marvel of making it to the top is the view, and gazing out as that Sinhalese king once did, surveying his magnificent domain. Well, perhaps: rumour has it that, after all the effort of constructing such a precariously perched redoubt, King Kashyapa was actually afraid of heights.

MAKE IT HAPPEN: Sigiriya is a 90km drive from the city of Kandy, which has bus and rail links to capital Colombo.

66

FANCY-FREE BACKPACKING, AUSTRALIA

It's an adventure for a gap year or a career break, a turning point in your life. Somehow, you have a month – maybe three months, or more – and nothing to hold you back. Australia beckons.

You hit Sydney or Melbourne, and get bowled over by kookaburras and flying foxes, surfboards and the Central Business District. You hire a car or a campervan, or jump on a bus, and head out: north onto Queensland's Barrier Reef coast, west along the surf-smashed Great Ocean Road, up through the Outback, or all the way over to Western Oz, with its vineyards and wild coastline.

You learn to be wary of 'roos and road trains, and what it really means to be hundreds of km from petrol or help, and how to pass the time on a 24-hour drive through nothing. You become part of the great gyre of Europeans spinning around 'Straya – the land of plenty truly has plenty to give.
MAKE IT HAPPEN: Hire a campervan from Maui (www.maui-rentals.com) or Britz (www.britz.com); or browse second-hand vehicles for sale at www.gumtree.com.

65

ROAMING THE REMAINS AT HAMPI, INDIA

There are plenty of ghost towns – but few that boast the otherworldly setting and atmosphere of Hampi. This sprawling World Heritage site in the state of Karnataka was once the capital of the mighty Vijayanagara Empire that stretched across southern India. As recently as the 15th century, it was ringed by 38km of walls and home to as many as 500,000 people – making it the second-largest city on the planet at that time and, according to contemporary travellers, one of the most magnificent sights in the world.

The city was destroyed in 1565 by the armies of the Deccan sultanates, but the remaining ruins are mesmerising to explore, set among weirdly shaped rocks and boulders. Several mighty monuments remain: the towering Virupaksha temple, somehow spared the annihilation and still an important pilgrimage site for Hindus, along with curiosities such as the intricately carved stone chariot in the Vittala complex. But most fascinating is to simply wander among overgrown bazaars and remote temples, imagining the bustling life that once flourished where now palms and bananas sway in silence.

Get here early, hire a bicycle (or a moped) and marvel at a city that was once said to rival Rome.
MAKE IT HAPPEN: Bangalore (Bengaluru) is the closest major hub with direct flights from the UK. Take the Hampi Express night train to the ruins. A cluster of low-key lodges and restaurants sit across the river from the ruins at Virupapur Gaddi.

64

LISTENING TO THE CREAK OF THE PERITO MORENO GLACIER, ARGENTINA

Glacier in not retreating shock! Patagonia's Perito Moreno is bucking the dismal global trend – this inching white tongue is just about maintaining its truly mammoth proportions (around 5km wide, 30km long) in the face of climate confusion.

It's so refreshing to read a nice ice story for a change. Indeed, everything about Perito Moreno is pretty refreshing. The glacier is the star attraction in Los Glaciares National Park, a vast wilderness of ice-capped peaks, sparkling lakes, cloud-racing skies and chuntering rivers that is invigorating enough to blow away anyone's cobwebs. This is the sort of landscape that will mess up your hair, clear out your nostrils and remind you that you are still alive.

There are several ways to experience Perito Moreno. Walkways and lookout points opposite the glacier give a distanced overview – a good way to see it in its full mountain-hugged context. If you're feeling energetic, specialist tours will equip you with crampons so you can actually walk on top of all that shifting ice, and hear it grind and groan beneath your feet.

Alternatively you can board a small boat and sail right up to Perito Moreno's terminus, to fully appreciate its scale: the blinding white-blue cliff looms up to 70m high, creakingly advancing into Lake Argentino. It's wise to keep a safe distance, though: every now and then the glacier heaves, and huge chunks – the size of trucks and houses – calve off with a crash into the chill water below.

MAKE IT HAPPEN: Los Glaciares NP is 78km from El Calafate, accessible by car or bus. Boat tours can be taken from Puerto Bandera.

63

YOMPING AROUND
YOSEMITE NATIONAL PARK, CALIFORNIA, USA

The granite grandeur of Yosemite is no secret. It wasn't the USA's first National Park (Yellowstone got that honour) but it certainly is one of the most famous. For it was here, back in 1864, Abraham Lincoln signed the Yosemite Grant, the first bill of its kind that was designed to protect wild land for everyone to enjoy for future generations. Many argue that this was instrumental to establishing it as a national park and indeed key to the formation of the creation of National Parks in North America (and the world) in the first place.

With further help from one John Muir in 1890, Yosemite became a bone fide protected national park and since then every year hordes of people descend on its riverside meadows, nostril-clearing pine forests and sheer rockfaces. But that doesn't stop it being jaw-dropping in aspect and fun to explore.

Ask any of the 3.5 million annual visitors what the Yosemite experience should be, and their responses will be as varied as the scenery that surrounds them; from a place to simply sit and commune with nature, to a high octane activity hub encompassing walking, camping and climbing – there are many reasons why people come to explore this mountainous, tree-lined valley.

But it's not just the landscape. Several large mammals including black bear, elk, deer, mountain lion and coyote call this place home. And for the best chance to spot them, you can't beat a hike in the backcountry, away from the tourist centres. With over 1,200km of designated trails amid the sweeping grandeur of alpine wilderness, groves of giant sequoias, deep glacial valleys and towering waterfalls, you literally are spoilt for choice. In fact one visit can't possible be enough to absorb the magic of Yosemite – but it's a start.

So grab your boots and map, and head into the wild hinterland, set up camp (there are more luxury camping options available now too), stash your comestibles in your bear locker and enjoy being a part of this wild place. Plan your trip for late summer or early autumn, when most areas of the park are still open but the crowds have gone home and the wildlife is most active.

MAKE IT HAPPEN: Yosemite is 314km from San Francisco. It's open year-round but some roads are inaccessible November-May. See www.nps.gov/yose

61

RAFTING THE ZAMBEZI, ZAMBIA

Victoria Falls – or, as its known in the local Makololo language, *Mosi-oa-Tunya*, 'The Smoke that Thunders' – isn't the world's tallest cascade, being a 'mere' 108m high. It's not even the widest, stretching about 1,700m. But it *is* the biggest, with the mighty Zambezi River forming the largest single sheet of water: at peak flow, up to 10 million litres of water crash over its lip every second – and you can imagine the torrent that creates in the narrow Batoka Gorge below.

For 120km the Zambezi squeezes through this narrow canyon, forming the border between Zambia and Zimbabwe – and, more importantly for adrenaline-junkie visitors, boiling up into the biggest sequence of Grade V rapids in the world. These seething maelstroms of whitewater have been given suitably violent names designed to tempt and terrorise: Oblivion, The Terminator, Washing Machine, Gnashing Jaws of Death. And they're just as daunting as the names suggest.

Even so, the Everest of whitewater can be tackled by a beginner – with the help of an expert rafting guide steering and shouting from the back. Jam your feet into the crevices of your inflatable, grab your paddle and pay close attention to the yells of your guide as you hurtle at white-knuckle speeds down the ferociously turbulent channel, or you'll tumble into the Zambezi – along with the hippos and the crocs...

MAKE IT HAPPEN: The best time to raft the Zambezi is between August and mid-October, when the water levels are falling – counter-intuitively, lower water levels mean wilder rapids. In November and December, the ride gets really hairy, and some stretches are unraftable. Half-, one- and multi-day rafting trips are available from operators in both Zimbabwe (Victoria Falls town) and Zambia (Livingstone).

62

SLOWING DOWN ON THE KERALAN BACKWATERS, INDIA

We love India for its high-energy, high-intensity mayhem, its constant barrage of colour, noise and people. But as fun as India is with the volume cranked up to eleven, sooner or later you need to turn it down and take a breather. That's where the Keralan backwaters come in. On a *kettuvallam* houseboat, floating along some of the 900km of lagoons, canals, rivers and lakes, a meditative calm descends and you can once again hear yourself think.

Meals are included on a standard cruise, and the quality is usually excellent. Make sure you try some of the local fish known as *karimeen* – it will be among the tastiest things you'll ever eat on the subcontinent. Then sit back, relax and enjoy the beautiful country at its most perfect pace.

MAKE IT HAPPEN: Domestic flights serve the city of Kochi (Cochin) from major hubs, including Mumbai and Delhi. Most backwater cruises depart between Kollam and Alappuzha; aim to stay at least one night on the backwaters. For info see www.atdcalleppey.com.

60
TAKING IN THE SUNRISE OVER **ANGKOR WAT**, **CAMBODIA**

For most travellers, it's the combination of beauty and scale that provides the wow factor for this remarkable temple, the principal monument in a city complex that includes Hindu and Buddhist temples in their hundreds. Most guides advise arriving early to catch the sunrise and miss the crowds, not to mention making the most of that famous view from across the moat, where Angkor Wat's ethereal double is reflected in the water.

After you've had your fill, hire a motorised bicycle and get 'temple bagging', being sure to tick off the south gate entrance to Angkor Thom, the Bayon temple with its proliferation of serene Buddha faces, and Ta Prohm, the atmospherically root-encircled 'jungle temple', along the way.

Angkor Wat's West Gate gets the lion's share of visitors, so opt instead for the quieter but no less impressive East Gate. By the time you're done ogling the stone temples basked in the warm glow of sunrise, the masses will have dispersed from the West Gate giving you the best of both worlds.

MAKE IT HAPPEN: Fly to Siem Reap from Bangkok or Hanoi.

59
PADDLING TO
ANGEL FALLS,
VENEZUELA

Canaima National Park, in south-east Venezuela, hard up against the Brazil and Guyana borders, feels positively prehistoric. Around 65% of the park is covered by *tepuis*, majestic, jungly flat-topped inselbergs that look like something out of *Jurassic Park* and have evolved in splendid isolation – from both the outside world and each other. This means the area is a hotbed of endemism, with each *tepui* summit harbouring its own unique ecosystem.

The most explored of these mountains is Roraima, which can be climbed on a steep and sweaty five-day expedition from the village of Paraitepui. However, this wildly remote, *Lost World* of a park is also a-splish with myriad waterfalls, not least Angel – the world's very highest.

Most of the world knew nothing at all about this record-breaking cascade until an American pilot named Jimmie Angel crashed on Auyantepui in 1937. The waterfall that now bears his name tumbles down the side of this *mesa* mountain and, with a drop of 979m, it makes Niagara look like your average garden water feature. From the *tepui*'s sheer walls, Angel plunges down at a thunderous pace in the rainy season; in the dry season – from January to May – it turns to mist before ever reaching the base of the Cañon del Diablo (Devil's Canyon) directly below.

Being buried in the jungle, Angel Falls is not easy to reach. The best way to experience it is to mount an expedition by dugout canoe, floating through lush rainforest,

before making a jungle trek to the vantage point of El Mirador de Laime. But it's as much about the journey as the destination. En route to the falls you might stop at indigenous villages to share *arepas* (corn cakes) and hunks of fresh pineapple with native Pemón people.

You might jump into glassy, vine-draped lagoons for cooling swims or shower under tumbling cascades. You might spy a bevy of birds flitting amid the trees and critters foraging in the undergrowth – there's plenty of wildlife in Canaima, including rarities such as giant anteater, giant armadillo and little spotted cat. You might picnic on pink-sand beaches and camp out by the riverbank, falling asleep to the sounds of frogs,

crickets and the rest of the rainforest orchestra. And you might be awed by views of the monstrous *tepuis*, looming above, swirled in a cloak of mist. If you're lucky you might glimpse a rainbow playing in the spray of Angel Falls itself.

After all this – a flight into the park, an expedition by boat (only doable when the water levels are right), and a sweaty jungle hike – you'll begin to appreciate why it took so long for something so very big to be found.
MAKE IT HAPPEN: From Caracas you can travel to Ciudad Bolivar by bus; from there the only way into Canaima National Park is to fly. Flights take about an hour and are an adventure in themselves, giving a bird's eye view over the forest below.

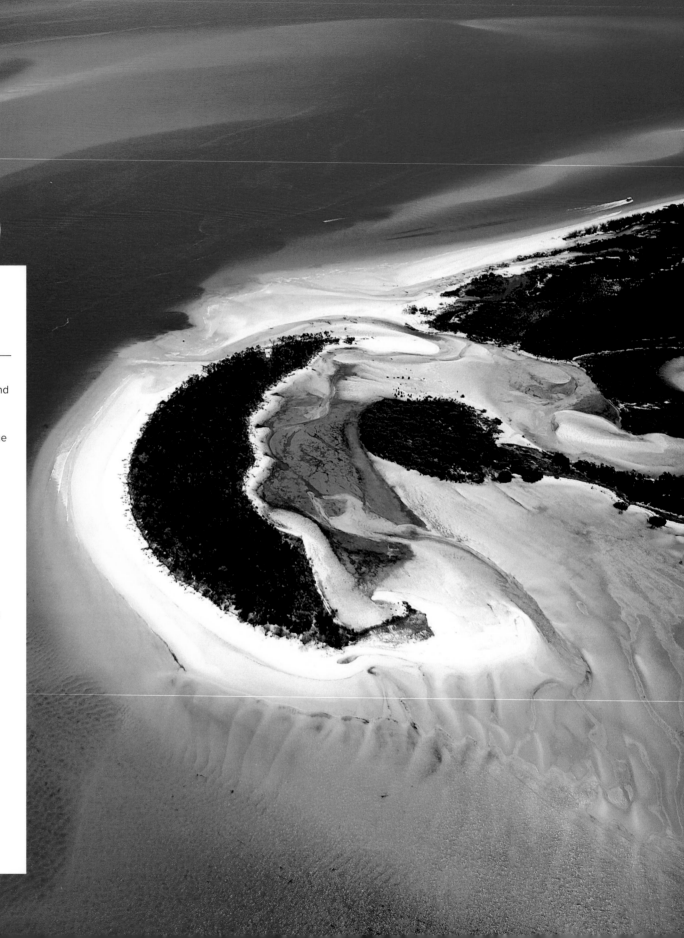

58

HAVING FUN ON FRASER ISLAND, QUEENSLAND, AUSTRALIA

Originally called Great Sandy Island (a name straight from the Aussie school of telling it like it is) this 123km-long wildlife sanctuary – the world's largest sand island – sits within Queensland's Great Sandy National Park. As you might have guessed by now, it's sandy. But more than this, Fraser feels like nature's theme park, a place where lakes, dunes and streams seem built for human fun.

Four-wheel drive across the beaches to access the 'rides' – Champagne Pools' fizzing surf, the dark depths of Lake Wabby, a gentle float with the fish down Eli Creek and the perfect-blue shallows of Lake Mckenzie. There are over 350 species of bird to tick off the list, too, as well as flora unique to the island. Just watch out for dingo looking to steal your campfire supper.

MAKE IT HAPPEN: Fraser is 15km offshore from Hervey Bay, 300km north of Brisbane. A 4WD is necessary to drive the island's beaches and inland roads; purchase permits before arrival.

56

SAMPLING SULTRY SALSA NIGHTLIFE IN
HAVANA, **CUBA**

Big, brash American cars (with Russian engines) straight out of the 1950s groan down the cratered streets as teenagers kick back on the sidewalk puffing on rolled cigarettes, too hot to do much more.

This is the timeless image of Cuba's capital and one that – due to the recent warming up of relations between them and their American neighbours, as well as promise of brand new direct flights from China to Havana coming soon – is causing travellers to descend on this most intoxicating Caribbean island in increasing droves. But there's still time to get there and experience a little bit of its old-time magic – and there's no better way to do that than going local and hitting the dance floor.

The evening, you see, is when Cuba comes alive, and nowhere more so than in the capital. Head to a salsa club when night falls and as you venture inside, through the clouds of cigar smoke, comes the unmistakable sound of feet stamping, hands clapping and dresses swishing up on the terraces.

Watch in awe as two women flick their hems and click their heels as they sashay back towards their partners – men wearing neatly positioned bowler hats and wicked smiles.

"*Aqui, aqui*!" they shout, and the women move towards them, mojitos in hand, while other Cubans holler and cheer, moving to the salsa beat. Now who wouldn't want to be part of that vibe?

MAKE IT HAPPEN: Most tour operators can arrange for you to participate in salsa classes on your visit. Caledonian www.caledonialanguages.com) can arrange salsa trips. Its two-week course involves dance lessons in Santiago de Cuba, with a chance to stay in a homestay in Havana – the best way to learn more about the country.

57

EXPLORING THE BACKSTREETS OF
KATHMANDU, **NEPAL**

It's one of those travel names – up there with Timbuktu and Marrakech – that exudes exoticism in its very syllables: Kathmandu, Kathmandu... You're itching to go before you even know anything about the place. And it doesn't disappoint. Despite the terrible earthquake that rocked the city in 2015, the Nepalese have worked hard to rebuild and send out the message that this is a place very much open for business. And it has intrigue aplenty...

Start amid the tiered-roof temples of Durbar Square – former seat of the country's monarchy and the old city's heart – before plunging off-piste, down alleys where dogs are decorated with marigolds, dim shrines flicker with butter lamps, prayer wheels spin, shops sell wool carpets alongside Gore-Tex jackets, and cafés serve mouthwatering cakes to old hippies, Everest summiteers and locals alike.

MAKE IT HAPPEN: Fly to Kathmandu, usually via India or the Middle East, then take a taxi (you can pre-pay a set price inside the airport to avoid haggling).

55

FEELING LIKE A MOVIE STAR IN NEW YORK, USA

The first time most people see the Manhattan skyline there is, ironically, something quite unreal about it. You've spent so much of your life looking at the virtual version through the medium of TV, cinema and advertising, you can't quite convince yourself that it isn't an elaborate film set or green screen mirage. But then this is precisely part of the thrill of the city.

On arriving here, you're immediately cast as one of the actors. Here you are in soft-focus taking a romantic stroll over the Brooklyn Bridge at sunset; now you're glamming it up amid the neon-lit fizz of Times Square perhaps taking in a show or two followed by some Manhattan cocktails; come the morning you'll be brooding heroically on a boat across from the Statue of Liberty and Ellis Island before ending the day strolling in the green expanse of Central Park among the joggers who look so perfectly preened you'd swear they just walked out of a commercial for shampoo or skin cream.

Then there are the museums, the art galleries, the pop-up restaurants, riding the subway, hailing a cab, visiting the new World Trade Center and the poignant 9/11 memorial, getting to the top of the Empire State Building and sneaking a peak at the Dakota Building and the John Lennon memorial – all quintessentially New York experiences.

And even the newer attractions have equally as much star appeal. Most recommended of them all is the High Line. Formerly a disused railway line, it's been transformed over the last few years – in what is gaining popularity in the USA as part of a 'rails to trail programme' where old abandoned tracks are being beautified for outdoor activity – and is now an elevated park filled with green lawns, wild flowers and open space and seating. It runs for just over two kilometres between the Gansevoort Street in the Meatpacking District to the south, up to West 34th street further north and offers views over the Hudson River and the city itself. It's also been a huge factor in regenerating some of the areas that it passes over and visitor numbers are increasing constantly, yet still it remains a very peaceful sanctuary above the busy yellow-cabs darting around like worker bees in the city that genuinely never seems to sleep.

Quite simply, no matter what your interests, from culture to adventure, there are more A-list attractions here than any city in the world. No matter when and where, the Big Apple always serves up a blockbuster performance. **MAKE IT HAPPEN:** Get to know the city through a local's eyes (for free) – go to www.bigapplegreeter.org.

54

APPLAUDING THE ATACAMA DESERT & EL TATIO GEYSERS, CHILE

There is a legend of a shepherd who was driving his sheep through a particular valley in northern Chile's Atacama Desert when he met the devil, who proceeded to lead them over a cliff to their deaths. That's why they call it the Valle de la Muerte. However, the 'Valley of Death' seems far too beautiful to have such a sinister past – especially when the wind-sculptured waves of pink rock take on a fiery hue in the late afternoon sun.

This pretty much sums up the whole of the Atacama Desert. It's a vast, strange expanse capable of bewitching any traveller that dares to pass through it – terrifying in its size and rawness, beguiling in its otherworldly beauty.

The Atacama region of Chile, which covers an almost incalculably large area of stony plains, sweeping sand, dazzling salt lakes and the barren lower slopes of the Andes, is one of the driest places in the world. Parts of it have seen no rain in living memory. The resulting landscapes are spectacular in their weirdness, often compared to Mars. This is especially apt, given that the extreme aridity and lack of clouds also makes for some of the world's best star-gazing – simply, nowhere else offers more dazzling night skies.

But there are pockets of green in the scattering of oases fed by underground rivers and meltwater from the Andes. San Pedro de Atacama is one such place, a little settlement established as a mission station by the Spaniards in the 16th century, and now a focal point for exploration of the area. It still feels like a frontier town with its single-storey adobe homes and sandy streets. The whitewashed church at its centre has a roof made out of cactus wood and a side-chapel devoted to San Isidro – the patron saint of rain.

From San Pedro it's easy to make forays out into the desert wilds. You can visit traditional Atacameños settlements, ancient rock art and the ruins of a 900-year-old hill fort where the Inca were defeated by the colonising Spanish. You can hike, bike or horse-ride into evocatively named places: the Valley of the Moon, the Plain of Patience, the Devil's Throat. There are volcanoes rearing up all over the place and lakes shimmering in unlikely colours, where leggy flamingoes flock to feast on algae.

Also nearby are the El Tatio geysers. Perched up at 4,300m above sea level, these spewing spouts are the highest geothermal field in the world. To best appreciate them you'll need to make an early start (a 4am pick-up from San Pedro is the norm). That's so you can make the drive across the pitch-black emptiness to arrive at dawn, when the blowholes send clouds of steam into the chilly morning air. It's a dramatic sight, the spray catching the golden rays, the water pooling all around in glassy puddles that reflect the warming sun rise. A magical start to the day.

MAKE IT HAPPEN: San Pedro de Atacama is 98km from the nearest airport at Calama. Aim to spend at least four days in the area, not least to adjust to the high altitude.

53

SWIMMING IN MARINE-LIFE HEAVEN, CAYE CAULKER, BELIZE

Some quote the fact that Belize boasts the world's second-largest coral reef, stretching nearly 300km along the eastern coast – but the size is hardly the point. Rather, consider the opinion of, say, Charles Darwin, who described it as "the most remarkable reef in the West Indies," or Jacques Cousteau, who named the reef's Blue Hole one of the top 10 dive sites in the world.

The real joy is that you don't need to don an oxygen tank to encounter its submarine denizens. At the northern end of the reef stretches a cluster of small islands, with fabulous snorkelling within touching distance. The pick of the bunch is probably tiny Caye Caulker, a laidback sandbar with world-class snorkelling just a short boat ride offshore. Float above the coral to spot countless technicolour tropical fish, toothy barracuda and big-mouthed groupers.

For even heftier specimens, take a boat trip to Hol Chan Marine Reserve and the aptly named Shark Ray Alley, where offcuts from fishermen cleaning their catch has created a veritable smorgasbord for nurse sharks and stingrays. Dive boats now feed the fish, and they swarm around in numbers – expect some very, very close encounters with 2m-long sharks. Elsewhere in the reserve, you might swim with turtles, rays, moray eels, kaleidoscopic fish and even dolphins.

Fewer people make it towards the southern end of the reef, but there's plenty to see here too, especially at the sheer drop-off at Glover's Reef Atoll and Gladden Spit where, between March and June, you could be lucky enough to flipper alongside mighty whale sharks.

MAKE IT HAPPEN: Reach Caye Caulker from Belize City by plane (15 minutes) or water taxi (45 minutes). The Caye is small enough to get around on foot.

52

ROAMING THE ANCIENT PYRAMIDS OF MEROË, SUDAN

Think pyramids, and you probably think Egypt or, at a push, Central America. Think again: on the eastern banks of the Nile in Sudan, some 200km north of Khartoum, stand the pyramids of Meroë, the great necropolis of the rulers of Kush. This powerful Nubian kingdom grew rich on iron-working, trading with lands as distant as India and China, and flourishing from around 800BC till its decline in the 4th century AD.

Here you can wander among dozens of sharp-pointed tombs that emerge from the sands in which they were buried for centuries, and delve into the funerary chapels lined with magnificent bas-reliefs – without the tourist hordes and camel-ride-touts that plague the larger monuments near Cairo.

MAKE IT HAPPEN: There are no direct flights from the UK to Khartoum; the fastest routes stop at Istanbul, Amman or Cairo. Operators including Wild Frontiers (www.wildfrontierstravel.com) and Undiscovered Destinations (www.undiscovered-destinations.com) offer guided tours.

51

GETTING YOUR MOTOR RUNNING ON
A ROAD TRIP, USA

When we think of the all-American road trip, it's difficult not to view it as a series of nostalgic vignettes: a cherry-red Chevy with the sound of Chuck Berry coming from the radio; a roadside burger joint straight out of an Edward Hopper painting; the neon sign for some remote church glowing with the promise of redemption. And the great thing is, you will find just this sort of thing (and much more) when you hit the highway. Sure, you'll hit the odd traffic jam, too, but whether you're thundering down Thunder Road in Georgia, driving through a preternatural Utah moonscape or breathing in the balmy air on the Pacific Coast Highway in Californ-i-a, what becomes clear is that America is never more itself than on the road.

MAKE IT HAPPEN: For route planning, see www.roadtripusa.com. Hiring an RV motorhome can keep down costs; try www.cruiseamerica.com. For general USA travel advice, check out www.discoveramerica.com

50

GLIMPSING THE PEAKS OF THE HIMALAYA,

BHUTAN, INDIA & BEYOND

Sometimes, no matter what anyone says to the contrary, size matters. And there's nothing bigger – nothing more slap-you-in-the-face, wobble-you-in-your-walking-boots, tremble-in-your-Gore-Tex awesome – than the high mountains of the Himalaya.

The entire range spans 2,400km, from Pakistan in the west to India in the east; much of it lords over 7,000m, some of it over 8,000m – a height not nearly approached elsewhere on the planet.

Literally translated as 'abode of snow' it can be no surprise that these high rising giants are plastered with a good, solid coating of the white stuff all year round. And the best part? Being so ludicrously big there's an abundance of ways to get up close and personal with them.

For the easiest option you can gaze in wonder at their impossibly sharp spires and buttresses from a distance in one of the Indian hill stations. For the more intrepid – and energetic – you can't beat exploring them on a trek. There are, quite literally, hundreds of options for hiking, from a simple wander to a multi-day trek or even a full on ascent of one of the still unclimbed peaks – yes, they actually have virgin summits here in the Himalaya (though climbing is strictly regulated by permit). And the accommodation options are growing too: visitors can choose from the budget-conscious camping, to local homestays, to nights in high mountain teahouses (usually consisting of a bed in a room – take your own sleeping bag – and a shared toilet) or more luxurious lodges with private bathrooms, proper duvets and hot running water.

For a taste of one of the most beautiful sections try remote Ladakh for a mix of verdant valleys, high passes, mountain monasteries and small, friendly villages. But you needn't grab your walking boots for a taste of adventure, simply take the white-knuckle flight into Bhutan's Paro airport – simply catching a glimpse of this range will take your breath away.

MAKE IT HAPPEN: Himalaya hub cities include Kathmandu, Lhasa, Islamabad, Paro, Delhi and Guwahati; take the train to Shimla from Delhi (via Kalka; approx 12 hours) for easily accessible views and to begin dreaming of all the possibilities these mountains offer the adventurous.

49
GOING ON A
BUSH SAFARI,
BOTSWANA

When choosing your next safari, you could follow a line of Jeeps across the savannah to crowd around a lion-kill or a cheetah on a termite mound, and be deafened by snapping cameras.

Or you could come to Botswana.

This landlocked country in southern Africa does things differently. Here, quality wins over quantity: with a government policy of 'high-cost, low-volume' tourism, visitors are guaranteed a safari experience unblighted by crowds. It's the connoisseurs' choice, and it's not cheap – but you get what you pay for.

And what is that? Well, a bit of everything: desert, delta, forest, big skies. Botswana has an amazing array of habitats, and the spectacular range of wildlife to go with it – the Big Five,

plus most of the other species you'd hope to spot in southern Africa. The choices of safari style are near limitless, too. You can gallop on horseback alongside herds of zebra, trek out in the bush on a walking safari, or canoe the Selinda Spillway, now flooded with water after 30 dry years and offering a unique paddling experience between the miraculous inland Okavango Delta and the Linyanti river system to the north-east.

That's the watery wonderland of the north-west – top of the wishlist for any traveller to Botswana. But head north-east and you'll encounter a different landscape: the thorny, sandy, part-wooded wilderness of Chobe National Park, where hefty herds of buffalo and elephant roam – probably

the highest concentration of the huge mammals in Africa. Or look south to the arid Kalahari, where the salt pans of the Makgadikgadi shimmer and game gathers at waterholes. Delve still deeper into the Kalahari to spot gemsbok, giraffe, cheetah and ostrich. Or hike among the abrupt outcrops of the Tsodilo Hills to discover galleries of rock art – thousands of paintings depicting those very creatures you've come to see, painted over many millennia.

MAKE IT HAPPEN: Botswana has some of Africa's most beautiful and luxurious lodges and camps, and most travellers book tour packages visiting these. But you can fly to Maun and pick up a safari, or plan a self-drive 4WD adventure, crossing the border from Zambia, South Africa, Zimbabwe or Namibia.

48

LIVING LOCAL ON
LAKE TITICACA, **PERU**

For the most authentic experience of
Lake Titicaca you can't beat
a homestay with locals. Start with
a trip to the floating Uros Islands, and
then on to Taquile to sample a local
dish of fried trout. Take time to look
round the craft market, which has
many woven products, all traditionally
produced. Then take a boat to one
of the tiny villages on the lakeshore,
where you will be introduced to
a local family in whose house you will
be staying for the night. Your new
friends will dress you up in traditional
costume and take you to the local
'hall' where you'll be treated to food,
drinks, and plenty of music and
dancing. Make time to visit Puno and
the Aymara tombs (called *chullpas*)
at Sillustani – massive, tower-like
structures on top of a plateau.
MAKE IT HAPPEN: Lake Titicaca's two
hub towns are Copacabana (Bolivia)
and Puno (Peru). You can arrange
homestays on the lake at either
of the two.

47

FEELING THE SPRAY, VICTORIA FALLS, ZAMBIA/ZIMBABWE

As the Zambezi River encounters the 1,700m-wide edge of the Victoria Falls gorge on the Zambia/Zimbabwe border it noisily and dramatically tumbles 100m into the depths below.

Be prepared to fall for the world's largest waterfall, as cascading torrents roar into deep plunge pools, producing giant clouds of misty spray, which glisten like diamonds in the powerful African sun.

Take a flight over the falls to truly appreciate their colossal scale or get next to the action: the best view from rim-level in the dry season is on the Zimbabwean side; hotspots in Zambia include Livingstone Island, the only accessible land in the middle of the falls — here, if you dare, you can take a dip in the Devil's Pool, and swim right up to the torrent's edge...

MAKE IT HAPPEN: Victoria Falls' water levels are highest April-June, but this is also the wet season; visit July-September for a good flow, but drier weather and better views.

46

WATCHING WILDLIFE IN ROYAL CHITWAN NATIONAL PARK, NEPAL

Most people think mountains when they think Nepal, but go to the right place and it's actually also a prime spot for wildlife watching. Introducing Royal Chitwan, a protected patch of Nepal's lowlands boasting 8m-high grasses and jungle scrub — the perfect hiding place and habitat for over 700 different species of wildlife.

Among the 43 different types of mammals recorded you could be lucky enough to see the orange-black flash of a Bengal tiger, the yellow-and-black spots of a leopard or the one-horned rhino. More likely though is that you'll spy an elephant, a sloth bear, a Bengal fox or a striped hyena, wild boar, hog deer, four horned-antelope.

But it's not just about the four-legged creatures. Look to the trees and you're sure to spot one of the over 500 species of bird. From white-throated kingfisher to paradise flycatcher and other winged wonders in between.

For those looking for more active pursuits, in addition to wildlife walks you can go on jeep safaris and head out rafting too.

MAKE IT HAPPEN: Chitwan is a six-hour drive from the frentic hustle and bustle of Kathmandu and is available to add on to many tours to Nepal and makes a fantastic addition to your post-trekking trip in the mountains. Go in January–March, after the long grasses have been cut, to have the best chance at wildlife viewing; June–September is very hot and wet.

44

STROLLING OLD CARTAGENA, COLOMBIA

One of the finest colonial cities in the Americas, Cartagena de Indias (to give it its full name) was once a strategic shipping post for the vast riches amassed by Spanish plunder. Today, much of the original walls (built in 1616) remain, topped by cannons and flagpoles. However, the true magnificence of Cartagena lies within the old Centro Histórico: stroll amid the attractive plazas, grand bubble-gum-hued mansion houses and charming cobblestone streets. In January, it's also home to the Cartagena Hay Festival, an exuberant literary shindig sometimes attended by local hero Gabriel García Márquez.

To get a great view over of old (and new) Cartagena, head to the hilltop Santa Cruz monastery. A taste of local life awaits at La Boquilla, a fishing village across town where empty rocking chairs sit outside homes with patchy paintwork and streetside barber stalls. One block away is the beach, largely deserted aside from flocks of pelicans nose-diving into the water, looking for lunch.

For more sun, sea and sand, you could head further east to the people-packed promenades of Santa Marta, but a little further down the road is a rougher-edged, tourist-free bit of trekking heaven: Tayrona National Park is a jungle-cloaked wilderness on the picture-perfect Caribbean coast, leading wanderers through the palm trees, prickly cacti and vulture-dotted grey boulders to isolated La Gomera and Arrecifes beaches. Keep an eye out for the elusive Kogi indigenous people who live in the Sierra Nevada.
MAKE IT HAPPEN: Colombia's dry season, or *verano* ('summer'), is December to March, with a second dry season June-August. Visitors typically fly in via Miami, New York, Panama City or domestic transfers.

45

MEETING MOAI, EASTER ISLAND, CHILE

When man is left to his own devices, the result, it seems, is to get big headed. Polynesians first arrived on the isolated, 164 sq km Pacific outcrop of Easter Island somewhere between AD 300 and 800 (no one's really sure). And here they stayed, unbothered by anyone else, until Europeans arrived in the 18th century. In that time, they got creative, constructing nearly 900 massive stone *moai* – long-faced figures, hewn from the soft tuff rock. Believed to represent ancient ancestors, these sacred spirits continue to watch over the island's beaches, volcanoes and cliffs today.

Many of the heads are mounted on *ahus* (plinths), some sport heavy top-knots and eyes of inlaid stone, many lay unmoved in the crater of Rano Raraku, the quarry where the *moai* were carved before being transported – somehow – around the island for purposes not quite known...
MAKE IT HAPPEN: Easter Island is 3,800km west of mainland Chile. Flights from Santiago take around five hours; onward flights to Tahiti are around five hours.

43

GETTING UP CLOSE WITH **RHINOS**, SWAZILAND

Two metres. Perhaps even a little less. That's how far away from you the dark, stocky, hunched body of a rhino could get before coming to a halt. When it happens, no one will dare move. Not a word will be spoken, not a breath drawn. He will eyeball you with suspicion but stand his ground while you study him from such close quarters that you could count the blades of grass stuck to his pointy horn.

After a few minutes the black rhino will lower his head and retreat, wandering back towards the dense thickets where others – perhaps a mother white rhino and her calf – wallow happily and safely in a freshly dug mud pool.

And that will be your introduction to one of the world's most beautiful and yet sadly endangered horned species – the rhinoceros.

To enjoy such a thrilling encounter, a great place to head to is the tiny Kingdom of Swaziland, a sovereign state in southern Africa. Grab yourself a ride in an open-topped Jeep and prepare to be utterly dumbfounded at just how often you can get such close proximity to one of Africa's most under-threat creatures in what the safari guides at the small, privately owned and funded Mkhaya Game Reserve call, "A bit of Mkhaya magic." This place is considered to be among the very best in Africa for rhino viewing.

You can even track them on foot. If you're brave enough. Take a morning's walk on the wild side to try and find one amid the shrill calls of bush babies. Watch monkeys swing in the treetops as you set off, following tracks sunken in the mud and filled with rainwater – your clue to their location. Eventually you'll stumble into a sweeping plain dotted with what looks like large grey boulders, which somehow – as if by magic – develop pointy horns and short stumpy legs. You'll have to keep your distance and be prepared to retreat at the word of your guide, but to watch these prehistoric creatures, standing on the same level as them, will be an experience that lasts a lifetime.

Rhinos have walked the earth for more than six million years, and, sadly, poaching is nothing new. Since at least the seventh century AD, there have been those who have thought rhino horns better suited to being cups and bowls. Today, the animals are hunted because those horns are considered medicinal in the Far East. Rhino numbers are in freefall around the world but in Mkhaya, somewhat of a refuge, things are looking up. The exact number is a closely guarded secret but rangers are locked in a daily – and sometimes deadly – battle against poachers armed with sophisticated means such as night vision equipment and even helicopters.

By far the best thing a traveller can do to help protect rhinos is go and see them: the more eyes on them the better for their fight for survival.

MAKE IT HAPPEN: Fly to Manzini via Johannesburg. Mkyaha Game Reserve is 55km to the east. For more info, visit: www.thekingdomofswaziland.com

42
GLIMPSING TORRES DEL PAINE, CHILE

It's not a friendly looking place. The sharp-shard peaks of Torres del Paine National Park, granite horns piercing the wilds of southern Chile, are fearsome – and often whipped by intemperate weather. But there's majesty and drama on a romantic scale in these mountains and for many they're the emblem of Patagonia itself. Head to the lookout of Mirador Ferrier, via a winding beech-lined path from Lago Grey, for a panorama of the whole massif. Or delve in proper: the 150km Circuit trail gets right in among the lakes, wildflower meadows, hanging glaciers – and those terrifying, awe-inspiring peaks.

MAKE IT HAPPEN: Weather is changeable year-round: December to March are warmest; October to November are best for wildflowers. The Circuit hike takes around 7-9 days, covering an average of 15-20km a day; hikers need to be relatively fit.

41

DIVING THE CENOTES, YUCATÁN, MEXICO

Poking like a thumbs-up into the Caribbean Sea, the porous Yucatán peninsula is something of a geological sponge. Its jungly interior, devoid of obvious lakes and rivers, is dimpled instead by thousands of soggy *cenotes* – sinkholes fed by underground springs.

Popular watery chasms include Ik-Kil (near Chichén Itzá), deep and inky Azul, and Kankirixche – atmospherically riddled with tree roots. To explore one of these crystal-clear hidden pools, often overhung by dangling vines and craggy cave-tops, is to combine swimming with spelunking. Dive in to float above stalagmites and strange rock formations, and to paddle with a fish or two.

MAKE IT HAPPEN: Swim sensitively: wear biodegradable sunscreen; don't touch or break off bits of rock; be wary of hitting stalagmites with flippers.

39

EXPLORING CAPPADOCIA, TURKEY

The creation of Cappadocia has quite some history: intense volcanic activity started it, and the Christians finished it off. Around 30 million years ago, Turkey's Anatolian plateau got carpeted in ash and lava, which gradually eroded into a hallucinogenic landscape of knobbly basalt chimneys and stripy tabletop mountains. The resulting landscape looks like something from a bedtime story or a very odd dream.

Then, around AD 600, early Christians on the hoof from the Arabs burrowed into the soft rock, creating underground homes, stores and monasteries – a great place to hide from enemy eyes. Whole subterranean cities were created, their churches decorated with colourful frescoes.

When you add together the handiwork of Mother Nature and Byzantine man, you get a unique cultural adventure playground. You can take hikes down valleys via weird rock formations and fairy chimneys; you can descend into the earth to inch down rock-hewn alleys and admire vibrant ancient art. And you can also drink excellent local wine, which has been made hereabouts for over 3,000 years.

Perhaps the best way to see superbly surreal Cappadocia is to hop into a hot-air balloon at dawn and float above it, gazing down on the natural turrets, crevices and canyons patchworking the plateau below.

For a different perspective, check in to a cave hotel – many of the traditional old dwellings carved from the rock have been converted into accommodation so that modern travellers can hide out like those Christians all those centuries ago.

MAKE IT HAPPEN: Kayseri is the gateway city – fly via Istanbul, or take the train. The laid-back village of Göreme is a good base for hikes and ballooning.

40

WHALE- AND DOLPHIN-WATCHING, NEW ZEALAND

Where waters collide – tropical hot and Antarctic chilled – so too do fish. And where fish gather, so too do mammals that like to eat them. Thus it is that the seas off New Zealand are a hearty stew of wildlife and, as such, the waves are thick with dusky dolphins, orca, humpbacks, sperm whales, even the mighty blue whale often puts in an appearance if you're very lucky.

Well-run boat trips will take you out amid the marine melée – you're practically guaranteed to see dolphins frolicking in your bow waves (and often you can even jump in to swim with them) before overhead spotter planes lead you to where the whales are, so you don't miss a fin-flick.

MAKE IT HAPPEN: Kaikoura (South Island) is a marine-mammal hotspot. Sperm whales are seen year-round; June-July is the best time to see humpbacks. It's also a great place to get the quintessential whale photo: a tail silhouetted against snow-capped mountain peaks – in this case, the majestic Kaikoura ranges.

38

GETTING UP-CLOSE WITH
ELEPHANTS, **SOUTH AFRICA**

There's a lot of Big going on in South Africa. For sure, the headline act is the famous Big Five – lion, leopard, buffalo, rhino and of course elephant – so named not just for their physical size but also because they were considered the most dangerous game for hunters. But at Addo Elephant National Park, the cast of colossi has been expanded: the 'Big Seven' also includes southern right whale and great white shark, both of which ply the protected waters off the Algoa coast.

In truth, though, there's only one encounter that will imprint indelibly on your memory. Picture this: you're standing opposite a young bull elephant that may or may not be about to charge. Even as a junior jumbo, it's very, very big – perhaps a third bigger than the Asian elephants you may have seen in Thailand or India. Your heart is pounding, the sweat is pouring, and you have some doubts about the effectiveness of your guide's placating tone of voice – you'd rather he got his rifle ready. All the same, you're locked into the moment, senses primed, alive in a way you've rarely felt before. The fact that you're on foot only adds to the electric frisson of the experience.

The most uplifting aspect of this encounter is that it's possible at all. When the park opened in 1931, a mere 11 elephants survived in the area – decades of intensive hunting had pushed them to the brink of extirpation. Now spanning about 1,800 square kilometres – making it the third-largest national park in South Africa – Addo is home to more than 600 elephants along with healthy populations of lion, leopard, spotted hyena and plentiful antelopes, plus more than 50 critically endangered black rhino. Thanks partly to the high density of elephants, they are largely habituated to humans and tend to be relaxed around vehicles – just as well, since you're likely to be halted by a column of big-trunked beasts crossing the road on a self-drive visit to Addo.

You'll also certainly watch comical warthog and big-horned kudu – both are amazingly common in the park – along with zebra, eland and the near-endemic flightless dung beetle, a local curiosity. If you're lucky, you could also see meerkats; for the phenomenally fortunate, there's even the chance of spotting caracal, aardvark and ardwolf.

If you want to get out and explore on foot, you can tackle the 32km, two-day Alexandria Trail in the Woody Cape section at the park's southern edge, or follow the shorter trails in the Zuurberg Mountains. Horseriding safaris are also available in some parts of the park.

However you roam Addo, though, keep your eyes peeling for a grey bulk with flapping lugs, and your ears open for a rumble and a trumpet signalling the arrival of the biggest of the Big Five. **MAKE IT HAPPEN:** Addo Elephant Park is 72km north of Port Elizabeth in the Eastern Cape. The park runs several camps and a number of luxury lodges operate in and around Addo. www.addoelephant.com

36

ROAMING THE OUTER HEBRIDES, SCOTLAND

Scotland's remote isles are the only places in Britain to make the cut here, a tribute, perhaps, to their other-worldly beauty. Cut off by the wind-whipped waters of the Minch, rural populations have expanded and collapsed over the centuries, but small-scale crofting endures today. From the expansive Lewis and Harris, to the flatter North and South Uists and Benbecula – all pockmarked by a smattering of lochs – to the smaller, stone-castled Barra, this entire archipelago forms a chain of some of the most rugged and wild-feeling landscapes you'll find anywhere in the world.

Ringed by some of the UK's loveliest white-sand beaches and crystal-clear waters – some of which are only accessible by foot – for a minute you'll have to pinch yourself as you'll swear you have actually travelled to the Caribbean. The marine wildlife will have you fooled that you're somewhere more exotic too, with whales, dolphins, porpoises and basking sharks all visiting at various times of the year.

Hikers, bikers and fans of wild swimming will find trails and opportunities for a dip galore, and without any of the hordes such beautiful scenery deserves. For something different – if you have the energy – you could take to the skies and kitesurf over Barra's beach airstrip, the only one in the UK. Or simply, pull up a deck chair and enjoy a beach all to yourself.

MAKE IT HAPPEN: Buy a rover ticket and island-hop on the Caledonian MacBrayne ferry (www.calmac.co.uk). May and September are great of good weather and lack of crowds. Avoid June-August to frustrate the dreaded Highland midge or at least take with you some Avon Skin-So-Soft, the only thing that seems to be effective against them (available in most gear stores).

37

VISITING AUSCHWITZ, POLAND

Great travel experiences aren't necessarily great fun. Take Auschwitz: you don't exactly enjoy walking through the eerie corridors and scrubby wastes of the former concentration camp, but it will certainly make a lasting and profound impression – which is what the best travel experiences should do.

The horror of what happened here during the Second World War still echo around the walls and hangs in the atmosphere of the place from the minute you enter; the cabinets full of used toothbrushes, Zyklon B canisters and human hair can't help but send shivers down the spine.

Most affecting are the long, long walls of prisoner-portraits, hinting at the true scale of the atrocity, and a step inside Gas Chamber 1, where many of those prisoners breathed their last. Haunting, memorable, and a absolute must for any traveller.

MAKE IT HAPPEN: Oswiecim (for Auschwitz) is on the Katowice-Kraków train line; Auschwitz 1 is a ten-minute walk or short bus ride from the station. See en.auschwitz.org.pl.

35

VISITING THE TEMPLES OF **BAGAN**, **BURMA**

Marco Polo called it "one of the finest sights in the world" as one of the world's greatest explorers, he should know. Once a thriving city of 200,000 people, Bagan is now a huge archaeological site, covering an area the size of Guernsey.

It's the sheer scale that astounds: the remains of 2,217 ancient stone temples, scattered across a vast, barren, copper-coloured plain. From the 11th to 13th centuries this 41 sq km complex was the biggest religious and cultural centre in the world. Now dusty and abandoned, what is left is best toured by bicycle or by horse and cart. At dawn and sunset the temples glow. The best views come from some of the lesser known temples such as Tha Kyas Hi, looking back across at the more photogenic Shwesandaw Paya and Dhammayangyi, and far from the hawkers and beggars that descend upon them.

There's more to Bagan than just its temples, though. There are villages, monasteries and mountains to explore. Follow in the footsteps of barefoot pilgrims and scale Mount Popa and cruise along the mighty Irrawaddy. **MAKE IT HAPPEN:** Bagan is 140km south-west of Mandalay.

34

CLIMBING SYDNEY HARBOUR BRIDGE, AUSTRALIA

Back in the day, bridge-climbing was generally the preserve of drunk university students. But you'll want all your faculties unimpaired for a hike to the summit of this particular structure.

Since it opened in 1932 the metal arches of the Sydney Harbour Bridge has become something of an iconic landmark both in its native Oz and across the globe (courtesy of it providing the backdrop to one of the most lavish New Year's Eve parties in the world).

You can easily walk across it, cycle across it, drive across it and sail underneath it, but this being Australia that simply wasn't enough. They figured, 'Why not climb it too?' And so the BridgeClimb experience was born.

You'll begin your ascent back in the Climb Base where you'll be kitted up in a flattering and specially camouflaged climbing jumpsuit and cap. You'll be secured into a harness, then shown how to clip in to the safety cables that are placed along the structure. After a few goes on a practice version with feet firmly on the ground it's time for the real deal and you'll head outside to get up close and personal with every nut, bolt and rivet of the bridge.

Watch how your legs wobble just a little as you take to the first of many ladders suspended above the fast moving traffic. Keep telling yourself not to look down as the seagulls swoop towards you to get a closer look, and try to hold a convincing smile when the Bridge Masters who accompany you up it stop you to take a photograph.

Some parts may be a little knee-trembling, but all the spent adrenaline will be worthwhile when you finally reach the distinctive Aussie flag that marks its highest point.

From here you can see Sydney Harbour from the most unique perspective in the city. You can pause for several minutes and plenty more cheesy photographs while taking in astounding views over the city. Gain a fresh perspective on the famous Opera House, the Botanical Gardens and The Rocks, and enjoy a bird's eye view of the Sydney city skyline.

As you climb back down to earth – and solid ground – feeling exhilarated from your climbing success, you'll notice the ferries whizzing by under your feet and the planes soaring overhead too. Then as you get closer to the road you'll take great satisfaction watching the tourists pointing up at you, remarking on how crazy/brave you must be to have climbed the Sydney Harbour Bridge – which of course you are.

The views are especially magical on the dawn and twilight climbs: these timings lend a tranquillity to the experience, as you watch the bustling metropolis come to life far below or wind down in the golden dusk.

MAKE IT HAPPEN: Guided climbs are offered exclusively by BridgeClimb Sydney. You can opt to go in the daytime for clear views; twilight to watch the city fade into dusk; or nighttime when the streetlights glisten beneath your feet. Go to www.bridgeclimb.com; early booking is recommended.

33

GETTING CLOSE TO MOUNT EVEREST, NEPAL

Given that it's the world's highest mountain – an 8,848m behemoth – Everest is surprisingly accessible. Not its summit perhaps: tough training, a qualified guide, a team of porters and high altitude Sherpas, supplementary oxygen, 70 days+ to spare and around £30,000 for a permit are just some of the things needed for that. But you can get amazingly intimate with the mountain in other ways: just 32km from Kathmandu, Nagarkot offers non-trekkers a breathtaking panorama, while short scenic flights from the capital can take you within touching distance of its summit.

To feel like a true mountaineer though, you should lace up your walking boots and take to the Everest Base Camp trail. It's a 14-day trek but the scenery makes the time fly by – you'll be surrounded by legendary Himalaya peaks so tall that the clouds sit below their summits and be staying en route in teahouses in traditional Sherpa villages where you'll learn just how important the Everest industry is to the local people. The finale comes when you reach the stupa and prayer flags of Base Camp – where many sleep at 5,364m, in the shadow of Sagarmatha.

MAKE IT HAPPEN: The dry season (October-May) is best for clear skies and is peak trekking season. Go in March-May to see the climbers preparing for their Everest ascent.

32

GOING WILD ON THE FALKLAND ISLANDS

To a generation, the name conjures up a war. But nearly 30 years after the Falklands conflict, Britain's south Atlantic islands are finally being appreciated for their natural assets.

Put simply, if you're into seabirds, you've hit the jackpot. Thousands of albatross, southern petrels and king cormorants ride the breeze, while down on the beaches platoons of king, gentoo and mohawk-sporting rockhoppers waddle while seals and dolphins appear among the waves.

Add in the brightly coloured Lego-like buildings of capital Stanley (complete with British telephone boxes, pubs and fish & chip shops), the moving memorials to the war-time dead and the sheer appeal of hopping between islands by light aircraft for around £25 a go, and you'll agree there's nowhere remotely like it.

MAKE IT HAPPEN: Three options: fly from Santiago, Chile; take the RAF flight from Brize Norton, UK; or join an expedition cruise; www.falklandislands.com.

31

WATCHING WILD ORANGUTANS, BORNEO, MALAYSIA & INDONESIA

Waiting in anticipation on the forest floor, you scan the lush green canopy above for a flash of orange. After listening in silence to the guide's orangutan calls for a few tense minutes, you suddenly lay eyes on these humanlike creatures as they make their long-limbed way to the fruit bonanza laid out especially for them. But although they are fed, make no mistake: these are wild animals.

Borneo's Sepilok Orangutan Sanctuary does rehabilitate orphaned apes, but it also provides a much-needed reserve for wild ones – the species, indigenous to Borneo and Sumatra, is endangered, and faces severe habitat loss. Sanctuaries such as Sepilok and the Semenggoh Wildlife Rehabilitation Centre in Sarawak are the easiest places to get a good glimpse; in the unfettered forest you'll need lots of luck – though forays in the unspoiled lushness of Batang Ai National Park and boat trips along the Kinabatangan River are perhaps the best ways to give it a try.

MAKE IT HAPPEN: Sepilok Orangutan Sanctuary is 23km from Sandakan, on Sabah's east coast; public buses run to within 1.5km of the sanctuary, or you can take a tour. Sepilok is open 9am-4pm; orangutans are fed twice daily, at 10am and 3pm. Pack binoculars; a fee is charged for using cameras/camcorders.

30
TEMPLE-GAZING AT
ABU SIMBEL, EGYPT

The most impressive aspect of the Sun Temple at Abu Simbel isn't its size or beauty – though with four 20m-high figures of Ramses II carved exquisitely from the rock, the mighty monument is both huge and magnificent – but that it was actually built twice.

Arguably the most dramatic of the ancient edifices along the upper Nile, the Sun Temple was originally carved from a cliff during the Ramses II's reign in the 13th century BC. Though dedicated to the gods Ra-Harakhty, Amun-Ra and Ptah, the most striking components are the four colossal statues of the great pharaoh that flank the entrance. Behind them lies a temple hewn deep into the mountainside, aligned such that the sun would penetrate the sanctuary only on the

king's birthday and the anniversary of his coronation. Nearby, a smaller (but still scintillating) temple dedicated to the goddess Hathor was built to honour Ramses' wife Nefertari, also featuring enormous statues of the pharaoh and his consort.

So far, so amazing. But the real miracle occurred in the mid 1960s, when the rising waters of Lake Nasser, created by the construction of the Aswan High Dam, threatened to drown the temples of Abu Simbel. To avert this cultural catastrophe, UNESCO organised one of the most laborious salvage jobs in history: the sandstone Sun Temple and smaller Temple of Hathor were cut up and relocated, block by block, to be embedded in a man-made mountain 61m higher up

a slope a couple of hundred metres from the original site. The operation cost the equivalent of about a quarter of a billon dollars today – but it looks like money well spent. The 33m-high facade, with its four huge statues of Ramses, continues to lord it over visitors just as it has for thousands of years.

MAKE IT HAPPEN: Abu Simbel can be reached on a day-trip from Aswan (by air or minibus) or aboard a multi-day cruise on the lake; it's also possible to spend the night in Abu Simbel town. Sound and light shows, usually held three times each evening, add another dimension to this ancient landmark. Time your visit for the early morning; though the temples are busiest then, by afternoon temperatures soar to scorching levels.

29
CATCHING YOUR FIRST SIGHT OF THE
TAJ MAHAL, AGRA, INDIA

What's the point of visiting the Taj Mahal? Sure, it's pretty. But you've already seen it from every angle, in every light, on a million postcards – what more is there to see? It's testament to the glory of this love-made-marble monument that this argument doesn't hold. Yes, it seems familiar, but the Taj – its graceful white curves, misty reflections, exquisite inlaid stone – does not disappoint.

You'll be fighting the crowds so make your first sight special: get to the gates for dawn, to be first in to watch as the mausoleum transforms

breathing 3D beauty under the rising sun. Take it all in but also take a closer look at its more subtle details: the intricate floral carvings and verses of Persian poetry on the walls.

Your first glimpse of this fabled mausoleum – built in the 17th century with a labour force numbering over 20,000 people – is a life-defining moment, so embrace the goosebumps as they creep along your arms one hair at a time.

MAKE IT HAPPEN: The Taj is open daily from sunrise to sunset (closed Friday); entry costs Rs750 (£10).

28
CLIMBING UP TO
TIGER'S NEST,
BHUTAN

Tucked into a mountainside in the west of a remote, long-isolated Himalayan kingdom is the cliff-face that launched a thousand postcards: the craggy eyrie on which the country's most famous monastery, Taktsang Goemba, perches. The 'Tiger's Nest' is Bhutan's Machu Picchu, its Angkor Wat – the spectacular sight that every visitor wants to experience.

Enjoying this view, though, is no doddle – and that's a big part of its charm. Several steep kilometres from the nearest road, the monastery is reached on a winding path that's perilously slippery in wet weather. The location doesn't make things any easier, either: the monastery sits at 3,120m, where the thin air is enough to leave you breathless.

But if the altitude doesn't have you gasping, the beauty of this dramatic spot will certainly take your breath away. The higgledy-piggledy, white-walled, gilt-roofed monastery, glimpsed between fluttering multi-coloured prayer flags, clings to the sheer rock face above lushly forested slopes. It's a photographer's dream.

You can venture into the monastery itself (make sure you dress respectfully, and prepare to leave cameras and mobile phones outside) but in truth the interior is possibly the least interesting aspect of the whole experience – destroyed by fire in 1998, the current structure was reopened as recently as 2005, and though the colourful paintings and statues inside are striking, it's the wonderful climb up,

atmosphere of the site and story behind its foundation that are the real draws.

The Tiger's Nest, you see, takes its byname from the route by which the great Buddhist Guru Rinpoche reached this spot in the 8th century AD. He flew here – on the back of a tiger, of course – to subdue a troublesome demon, after which he meditated in a cave for three years. The original monastery was built above that cave much later, in 1692, and was anchored to the cliff face by the hairs of female celestial beings. Or so the story goes.

That tale – and the monastery itself – encapsulate all that's most wondrous about Bhutan. It's a land that cherishes tradition like no other – and Taktsang is the best place to learn about its unique and mesmerising culture.

MAKE IT HAPPEN: Visiting Bhutan is possible only on an organised tailor-made or group tour, including all accommodation, transport and guides. The country's only international airport, at Paro, is served by flights from Kathmandu, Delhi, Kolkata and Bangkok. It's also possible to arrive overland from India.

Taktsang Goemba is 10km north of the town of Paro. The road ends at 2,600m; it's a one-hour walk up the trail leading from the car park to a café and viewpoint, and there's a further steep climb to the high observation point (3,140m) and across to the monastery itself. If your legs aren't up to the long haul up, horses and mules can be hired for the climb to the café.

27

WHITEWATER RAFTING, NEPAL

Prepare for a dunking. Running straight off the world's highest mountains, it's no wonder Nepal's rivers pick up a bit of speed. The country is a-froth with rapids of varying ferocity that not only offer an adrenaline shot to the intrepid, but access to glorious gorges and riverbank camps impossible to reach by other means. The Trisuli River is near Kathmandu, ideal for the time-poor, while the Kali Gandaki, nearer Pokhara, is wilder with fine peak views. For a frontier feel, head out west to the Karnali – eight-day expeditions offer tough rapids, dramatic and unspoilt scenery and, ending in Bardia National Park, perhaps a rhino, croc and tiger or two.

Those who like their adventures a little tamer are also well-catered for. The Seti River, which links the scenic lakeside town of Pokhara and Royal Chitwan National Park and eventually flows into the Ganges, is ideal for nervous first-timers with a series of Grade Three rapids spread along a 22-mile stretch that starts in the foothills of the Annapurna Mountain range.

Best of all, the overnight voyage (rafters set up camp on a quiet spot beside the river) reveals a slice of central Nepal that few see. Spot Himalayan barbets and electric blue kingfishers as school children shout 'Namaste' from the embankments.

Other of Nepal's rivers slice through deep gorges and showcase spraying waterfalls and remote tribal villages meaning not all the thrills here come courtesy of the foaming white water rapids. Just try not to scream too loudly.
MAKE IT HAPPEN: Rivers are dangerously fast at the height of the monsoon (July-August); the best time is October-November, when water is fast but manageable by novices. Different rivers have different peak times – make sure you check before booking.

26

SEEING A SOLAR ECLIPSE, VARIOUS

Most of us at one time or another have squinted through a pinhole in a piece of cardboard or donned a pair of particularly dark glasses to get a look at a solar eclipse. But there are those – numerous enough to have spawned the collective moniker of 'umbraphiles' – who are eclipse-chasers, traversing the globe in search of total solar eclipses (which come around every 18 months on average, although partial eclipses are far more common).

Travellers journey to some of the furthest flung corners of our planet to watch this cosmic drama play out from that year's best vantage point – from Bhutan to Easter Island, Tenerife to Turkey. Find out when and where you can next see this incredible phenomenon and pack your heaviest shades.
MAKE IT HAPPEN: A number of specialist tour operators run trips combining eclipse-watching with some soft adventure. For more information of upcoming eclipses, check out www.timeanddate.com.

25

SPICING THINGS UP ON ZANZIBAR, TANZANIA

Your full-sensory experience of the spice island of Zanzibar starts at the harbour, when you first catch a whiff of nutmeg and cinnamon stacked in hessian sacks on the dock, and it continues throughout your stay. Watch the sunset while cradling an icy beer as lateen-sailed *dhows* float by. Taste the deliciously fresh seafood, sizzling on barbecues under the light of hurricane lamps in Fordhani Gardens. Listen to the children playing in the maze of dusty lanes that form the heart of Stone Town.

When life in Stone Town gets too 'hectic', head to the beaches. Nungwe offers sugar-white sand, but the east coast is quieter, and allows you to cross the interior, brimming with the spices the island is famous for.

MAKE IT HAPPEN: Fly to Dar es Salaam, and then take a boat or a prop-engined plane to the island. Many visitors combine Zanzibar with climbing Kilimanjaro or a Tanzanian safari.

24
ROCKING OUT IN **UTAH'S** CANYONS, USA

Utah's majority Mormon population arrived in the state about 150 years ago. They took one look at the dreaming spires, flying buttresses and vertiginous vaulting hewn out of the rock by nature herself, and felt compelled to make it home. Native Americans had, of course, revered this strange and beautiful land for millennia before the arrival of European settlers – evidenced in the rock art dotted throughout the state, which speaks of the alchemical power of this landscape to transfix and elevate the spirit.

The national parks of Zion and Bryce Canyon are the most popular and, beyond simply gawping, are great for hiking, adventure sports and wildlife – you'll see coyote, mule deer, bighorn sheep and, if you're really lucky, mountain lion.

MAKE IT HAPPEN: Fly to Salt Lake City. Hire a car and use Utah's Scenic Byways to link the parks; see www.utah.com.

23

ISLAND-LOUNGING, MALAYSIA

Malaysia's less celebrated east coast idylls, Tioman and the Perhentians, remain popular with visitors in the know. Most famous for their natural beauty, these coral-fringed islands offer lush forest scenery, unspoiled white beaches and plentiful opportunities for snorkelling and scuba diving in their pristine turquoise waters.

Get hands-on with green turtle conservation projects on the beaches of Perhentian Besar, or stretch your legs on a short trek through inland jungle brimming with wildlife including exotic birds, monkeys and giant monitor lizards.

MAKE IT HAPPEN: The Perhentian Islands can be accessed by boat from Kuala Besut, about 110km north of Kuala Terengganu. Ferries to Tioman run from the east coast town of Mersing.

21
GOING WILD IN KAKADU NATIONAL PARK, NORTHERN TERRITORY, AUSTRALIA

Kakadu *is* Australia. This vast national park (at 20,000 sq km, the country's biggest) is the sweltering Outback, croc-infested wetland, roo-hopped scrub and ancient art-daubed rock of your most vivid Oz imagination. Here, cliché becomes spectacularly three-dimensional; you can feel millennia of red dust and Aboriginal history hanging in the air.

There are plenty of reasons for visiting. Those rock art sites are fascinating, featuring naturalistic and 'x-ray' images of animals and humans painted up to 20,000 years old — head for Ubirr, Nourlangie or the less-visited Nanguluwur site to admire those prehistoric pictures.

There are tremendous walks to spectacular waterfalls where you can cool off in the spray: Jim Jim Falls plummet 215m, while Twin Falls — as the name suggests — offer twice the fun.

But the main draw is the wildlife. Crocs lurk in those rivers and pools — the terrifying saltwater species grows up to 7m long, with correspondingly huge teeth. There are plenty of less-daunting animals to spot, too: dawn and dusk are good times to watch bats and wallabies, while a boat trip on Yellow Water Billabong reveals a wealth of birdlife.

Alternatively, unroll your swag, bed down for the night and simply listen: to the dingo's howl, the barking owl and untold unknown rustlings beyond...

MAKE IT HAPPEN: Kakadu is a three-hour drive from Darwin. Some areas are inaccessible in the Wet (October-March); the best time for wildlife watching is June to mid-August. For information on planning your trip, details of tours and accommodation and to buy a park pass visit www.environment.gov.au/parks/kakadu

22
WALKING WITH THE ANIMALS IN SOUTH LUANGWA NATIONAL PARK, ZAMBIA

Staring into the baleful yellow eyes of a male lion is a spine-tingling experience. But when you're on foot, without even the metal door of a vehicle protecting you from this magnificent predator, the sensation is simply electric.

That's what you get in Zambia's South Luangwa National Park, birthplace of the walking safari. Intimate encounters with wildlife – elephants, endemic Thornicroft giraffes and those beautiful lions – are nigh guaranteed, but Africa's best guides bring every tiny member of the animal cast to vivid life. Who knew an elephant shrew could be as enthralling as an elephant, an antlion as impressive as its feline namesake?

This is one of the best places in the world to see leopards, too, and African wild dogs roam the park. With thrilling night drives and beautiful lodges and camps, South Luangwa arguably offers Africa's best safari experience.

MAKE IT HAPPEN: Mfuwe is the gateway to the national park, with daily flights from Lusaka and Livingstone.

20
SOAKING UP **SANTORINI**, **GREECE**

Romance out of cataclysm – that's Santorini's story. Four thousand years ago, this mini-archipelago in the Cyclades was a single fertile island known as Strongyli ('the circular one') home to a thriving civilisation influenced by Minoan Crete to the south. The island was more than just an island, though: it was a huge volcano, long dormant – but not extinct. Around 1640BC, it erupted with probably the biggest explosion in recorded history, spewing forth a column of ash reaching 36km high and sending vast volumes of magma flooding down its slopes. The centre of the island collapsed, filling with sea and leaving only a craggy, sheer-sided caldera ring above the azure waves.

What remains today is pure Greek-isle fantasy: whitewashed houses crammed onto the rim of the caldera, steep-stepped switchback alleys leading down to old harbours, and traditional tavernas serving fish suppers. The volcanic soil has other benefits – Santorini's vineyards produce excellent wine. In short, Thira – as the main island of Santorini is officially known – is your dream Mediterranean idyll.

Unsurprisingly, it's a dream shared by plenty of other people. Come in summer and you'll encounter hordes; the island's permanent population is only around 15,000, a number swelled by some half a million visitors each year.

But though the commercialisation of the island can't be denied, neither can its beauty. Whether you're watching the sparkling waters in the central caldera from the main town, Fira, or one of the smaller settlements such as Oia, it's hard to begrudge your fellow admirers.

And there's more to see around the island of Thira. The Minoan settlement of Akrotiri, buried by ash during the eruption of the 17th century BC, is being excavated – you can wander among its streets and squares, and admire its frescoes now preserved in the Museum of Prehistoric Thera in Fira. There are Hellenistic, Roman and Byzantine ruins at Ancient Thira, and tempting beaches – albeit with black or greyish sand – at spots such as Kamari, Perissa, Vlihada, Monolithos and Red Beach, with its intriguing rock formations. Several wineries offer tastings, too.

A few other fragments of the volcano are worth a visit. A patch of the caldera's western rim is now the island of Thirasia, a low-key, unspoiled alternative to Thira, its main clifftop settlement Manolas is home to just a couple of hundred people.

Rising from the sea in the centre of the caldera, two small islets are still volcanically active; on a day trip you can visit the hot springs on of Palia Kameni and see rumbling Nea Kameni.

Mostly, though, Santorini is about the views from Thira – or, rather, one particular view: the sun setting into the waters of the caldera, best enjoyed with a sip of the island's fine white wine.

MAKE IT HAPPEN: Ferries connect Thira with Piraeus (for Athens) and other islands including Crete, Mykonos, Ios, Naxos and Paros. Domestic flights serve Santorini airport from Athens.

9

BEING BEWITCHED BY THE **NORTHERN LIGHTS, VARIOUS**

hey are the spirits of dancing
 Finland they are known as
let or 'fox fires' from a fable
ature sweeping snow
ith its tail. The Algonquin
ught they were Nanahbozho
 lighting fires as a reminder of
ove. Myth and mystery have
ed the aurora borealis aka
 Lights.

know their origins are more
ey're not heroes battling or
 of the dead but rather the
nospheric gases crashing
d particles from the sun.
vay by solar winds, these
 largely deflected by the

earth's magnetic field. But the field is
weaker at the pole, so particles sneak in
and collisions occur. The result: a celestial
spectacular above our planet's extremes.
Colours vary. Most common is yellow-
green, produced by oxygen molecules
bumping about 100km up; rarer red
displays result from collisions at 300km.
But knowing the science doesn't matter
– when you see the glimmer for
yourself, you'll still believe in magic.
MAKE IT HAPPEN: Good places to see the
northern lights include Svalbard,
Tromsø (Norway), Kiruna (Sweden),
Yellowknife (Canada) and Wiseman
(Alaska). You can even do a course in
Churchill, Canada (churchillscience.ca).

18

CLIMBING TABLE MOUNTAIN, CAPE TOWN, SOUTH AFRICA

Not one for the indecisive, there are more than 350 routes to the top of Table Mountain – such is the lure of the squat, cloud-shrouded monolith that lords it over Cape Town and the Atlantic beyond. The route that you choose depends on your skill level: some of these options are for experienced climbers only but thankfully many are manageable by more casual walkers.

The Platteklip Gorge trail follows the route taken by the first explorers to conquer the peak and remains the easiest way up to its 1,086m high point (aside from the cable car, of course). The Pipe Track, from Kloofnek, is a picturesque alternative, skirting the massif's western flanks, giving visitors gorgeous views of the sea.

MAKE IT HAPPEN: Visitors to Table Mountain National Park must pay a standard conservation fee on entering: R110 a day for adults, R55 for children. www.sanparks.org/parks/table_mountain

17

SAILING OUT ON MILFORD SOUND, NEW ZEALAND

Don't be in a hurry to get to Milford Sound: the journey to this remote geological masterstroke is an experience in itself. Grab yourself a car and drive to it via mountain-carved Milford Road, a real rollercoaster of a route in, punctuated by so much scenery you'll struggle to cover ground fast – endlessly stopping to take yet another photo. Or you could head in by plane, flying in over the serrated peaks of Fiordland – equally as impressive as the arrival. By the time you get to Mitre Peak, which lords over the Sound's head, you'll already have been treated to some of New Zealand's best bits. From there you can take your pick of the cruises that sail out into the fiord pass.

As you glide over the water you'll be seemingly surrounded by steep rock faces on all sides, carved by ancient glaciers. Not only is the mountain scenery epic but you'll see your fair share of charging waterfalls too, not to mention the local residents: fur seals, dolphins and little penguins among them. To have an unforgettable experience, book an overnight sail to drop anchor in a remote cove, for a magical Sound sleep.

MAKE IT HAPPEN: Milford Sound is a 2.5-hour drive from Te Anau or a 35-minute scenic flight from Queenstown. For more go to www.fiordland.org.nz.

16

WALKING THE GREAT WALL, CHINA

The challenge of walking the entire length of the Great Wall of China is, frankly, a pretty insurmountable one. Not only would it be an immense distance – nearly 9,000km, according to some surveys, snaking from Xinjiang in the far west to the Yellow Sea at the border with North Korea – but there's a bigger quandary to address before setting out: which wall would you walk?

The Great Wall, you see, isn't just one barrier, but many. A first series of defences were constructed in what's now Shandong province by the Qi and Chu kingdoms in the 7th century BC, with another chunk erected in today's Shaanxi province by the kingdom of Qin in the 5th century BC.

It wasn't till 214 BC that Qin Shi Huangdi – the 'First Emperor' whose tomb was guarded by the vast Terracotta Army – ordered the creation of the first truly 'great' wall (defined as being over 5,000km long); perhaps a million workers laboured, and probably died, in its construction. Later Han, Wei and Jin rulers built further sections.

It was the Ming dynasty, though, that was responsible for much of what we now recognise as the Great Wall, erected from the 14th century after the Mongols were ousted from China. Whereas many earlier walls were rammed-earth barricades running between the natural defences formed by mountains, the Ming wall comprised long stone and brick sections with crenellated fortresses and perhaps 25,000 watchtowers. This wall was many metres high and wide enough for horses to ride along its top; this is the barrier you picture when you imagine the Great Wall of China.

Many parts of the wall are now little more than crumbling piles of mud – fascinating historically, but hardly photo-album material – while some stretches hint at its former grandeur. Conveniently, most of the best-preserved (or restored) sections are near Beijing.

The most popular is at Badaling, which tends to be thronged with masses sporting 'I walked the Wall' T-shirts. But despite the crowds, and even though it's been heavily restored, this is among the most impressive sections – almost 8m high and 6m across. Mutianyu is another well-restored section with imposing guard towers; it's a little farther from the capital, so welcomes smaller crowds.

For a thrilling wall walk, though, head to the Jinshanling stretch near the town of Gubeikou. From here, it's a spectacular 10km walk to Simatai, winding through the mountains; plenty of towers punctuate the wall like pearls on a very, very long necklace.

And no – you can't see the Great Wall from space.

MAKE IT HAPPEN: Gubeikou is a three-hour drive north of Beijing; the 10km walk along the Jinshanling stretch to Simatai takes four to five hours. Simatai itself offers snapshot-friendly views of the Wall clinging to Yanshan Mountain. Badaling is 70km from Beijing, Mutianyu 90km; buses to both take less than two hours from Beijing.

15 SNORKELLING WITH RAYS IN BORA BORA, FRENCH POLYNESIA

Rarely has a creature been less aptly named than the 'devil fish'. The manta ray may be immense – 5.5m across, weighing nearly a tonne and a half – but it's completely harmless (unless you're plankton) and angelically graceful, gently flapping those 'wings' to glide and swoop through the turquoise-tinted waters of the South Seas.

Even angels' wings need grooming, though – and that's where the cleaner station on the reef at Anau, in the lagoon of Bora Bora in French Polynesia, comes in. The behemoths head here to have parasites picked from their skin and gills by cleaner wrasse and other small fish. Sounds icky, but it's a jaw-dropping spectacle.

You can bag a front-row seat at this aquatic ballet, gawping as half a dozen vast rays queue to be nibbled clean at the station, where sightings are virtually guaranteed. There's no need to don scuba-diving gear – the site is shallow, so a mask and snorkel is all you need: simply drop into the bath-warm, azure waters and wait for a graceful giant to glide silently by.

There's much more to see in this underwater garden, too, including several other ray species – don't be surprised if you bump into a bat, sting, leopard or eagle ray – as well as profuse black-tip reef sharks and a kaleidoscopic array of tropical fish: rainbow-hued parrotfish, spindly trumpetfish, spotty pufferfish and many hundreds more.

And the 'devil fish' moniker? That unfortunate byname comes from those horn-like cephalic lobes that help funnel plankton into the manta ray's gaping maw.

MAKE IT HAPPEN: Bora Bora is 250km north-west of Tahiti. Daily flights from Tahiti's Faa'a airport take 50 minutes. There are also regular boats to Bora Bora from Pape'ete in Tahiti.

14
WILDLIFE-WATCHING IN
THE MASAI MARA & SERENGETI,
KENYA & TANZANIA

What makes the Great Migration great? Partly it's the almost unimaginable numbers – some 1.5 million wildebeest, plus half a million Thomson's gazelle and perhaps 200,000 zebra, all of them trundling on a vast carousel through the 24,000 km sq Greater Serengeti ecosystem. That's a *ss* of ungulates.

Mostly, though, it's the drama: the synchronised birth of tens of thousands of wildebeest in the southern Serengeti in February; the prides of lions stalking their prey across the savannah; the massed ranks of herbivores charging across the Mara and Grumeti rivers between June and September, picked off by snapping crocodiles as they attempt the hazardous crossing.

But even if you don't time your visit for one of the key episodes, there's thrilling wildlife-watching in any season in both Kenya's Masai Mara National Reserve and Tanzania's Serengeti

National Park. This is the quintessential safari experience: rolling savannah punctured with rocky outcrops and acacia trees, a smudge of distant hills, and the biggest of African skies.

There are predators galore: the Mara, is known for its lions, most famously the Marsh Pride, stars of the BBC's *Big Cat Diary*. Elusive leopards hunt here, too, along with spotted hyena and cheetah – the sight of this lithe sprinter atop a termite mound is among Africa's most iconic images. The Big Five are all here, in fact – add buffalo, elephant and critically endangered black rhino – as well as diverse birdlife, and opportunities to meet the local Maasai people.

MAKE IT HAPPEN: Fly to Nairobi (Kenya) or Arusha (Tanzania). Pick up a safari locally, or pre-book with a specialist tour operator. Staying in one of the adjacent conservancies offers chances to enjoy night drives and walking safaris.

13

CLIMBING KILIMANJARO, TANZANIA

Whether you rate a schlep up Africa's highest mountain as a 'great travel experience' depends largely on when you're asked. Question the climber rising at midnight to make the final push to the summit – an ascent from 4,000-ish metres to that longed-for success sign at 5,895m – and they'll likely say not. At that moment it's a tough, cold, thin-aired, boring, nauseating, exhausting hell-on-high.

But ask that same soul about six hours later, when they're grinning like an idiot on the roof of a continent, with the clouds spread out beneath their feet like feather blankets and the answer will be very different indeed.

As the most accessible of the world's Seven Summits (highest mountains of each of the seven continents) it's also the most popular so choose your route carefully to ensure less crowds.

MAKE IT HAPPEN: There are five main routes up Kilimanjaro: Machame, Marangu, Lemosho/Shira, Rongai and Umbwe. Climbs take 5-9 days; longer treks allow better acclimatisation.

12

SEA-KAYAKING WITH ORCA, CANADA

Vancouver Island is a natural beauty. Situated not far from the city with whom it shares its name, it has earned an enviable reputation for chilled-out locals and spectacular scenery. Happily it's also one of the best places in the world to see killer whales, aka orcas – meaning a visit here at the right time of year can mix excitement, relaxation and wildlife encounters in glorious fashion. There are resident pods that live in these waters year-round, not to mention humpback whales too, but they are joined in the summer by many others, as they congregate in Johnstone Strait to feast on salmon.

You can sometimes hear these black and white giants before you even see them: listen carefully for sound of the whoosh of air as they draw breath before diving. Or you'll see the distinctive shape of the huge dorsal fin of an adult male as he slices through the water, and then with a growing sense of delight realise that there is in fact a whole family pod there with him, including babies sticking to their mother's sides. Out on the water, you in your flimsy-seeming kayak, you realise just how big and powerful they are. If you're lucky you may even get to see one breach – or at least splash you with their powerful tail.

MAKE IT HAPPEN: June to October offers the best chance to spy for orcas. Fly to Vancouver, then take the ferry to Vancouver Island; there are plenty of local outfitters who can arrange kayaking trips. Go for as long as you can to ensure plenty of attempts to see these beautiful marine mammals.

11

APPRECIATING ALL THAT ICE
ANTARCTICA

No matter where you've travelled to before, regardless of how much time you've spend in snowy places – skiing, walking or watching the northern lights – nothing, but *nothing*, prepares you for the beauty and sheer volume of the ice you'll find in the Great White Continent. Effort is required to get there – effort and sea legs: the notorious sail to Antarctica across the Drake Passage can be a tough one and, over the two days it takes to navigate, you may question if it's worth it... but then you arrive and that is swiftly forgotten as you start to see more

and more 'bergy bits'. From giant lumps that bang off the side of your ship to the enormous tabular variety that tower higher than your vessel itself, each one will have you at a loss for words.

Of course, the wildlife is a reason to go to Antarctica too: the various penguins steal your heart while sightings of whales, leopard seals and snowy shearwaters will make any trip memorable. But it is the scenery, and the patterns, textures and colours of the icebergs – astonishing blues, greens, turquoises so clear and piercing – that

are unexpected and will have you acknowledging that man can't design anything as beautiful as Mother Nature can. Most go thinking it's a once in a lifetime experience, but as the peninsula slips away when you depart, you secretly hope one day to come back for more.

MAKE IT HAPPEN: Expedition cruises leave from Ushuaia (Argentina), Christchurch (NZ) and Hobart (Tasmania), ranging anywhere from 10 days to 3 weeks. Look for smaller ships so that you'll get the most landings.

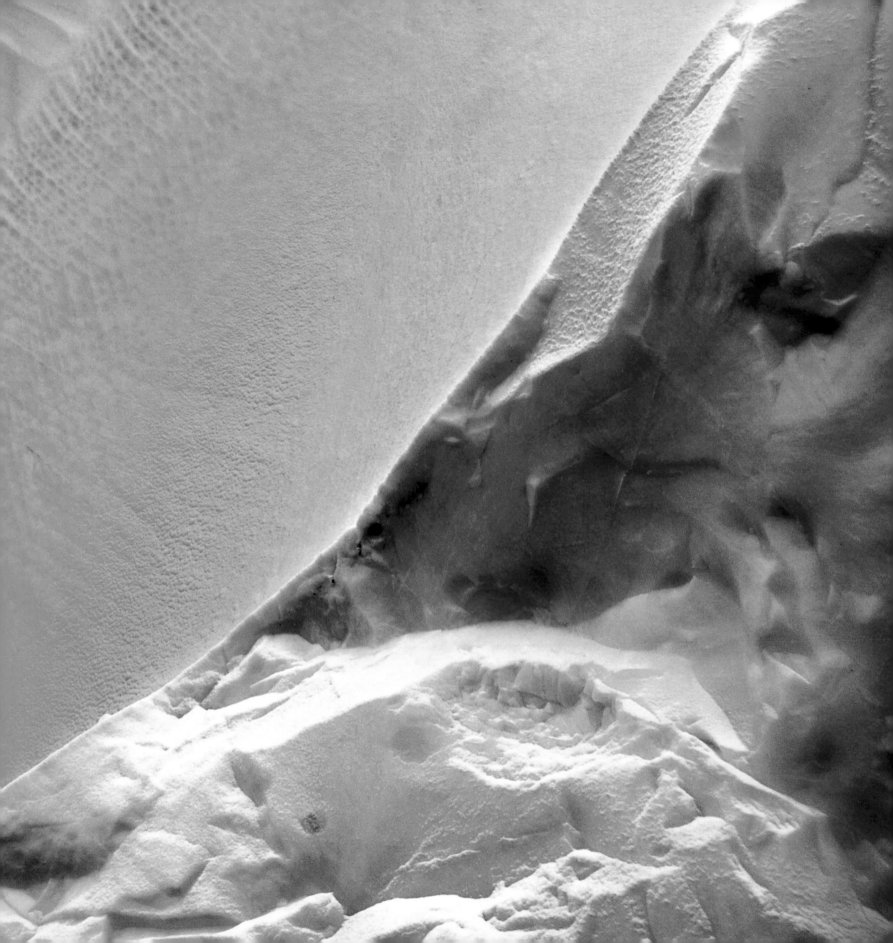

10

GETTING YOUR FIRST GLIMPSE OF ANCIENT PETRA, JORDAN

Cue the *Indiana Jones* music... ever since Harrison Ford, Sean Connery and co galloped through the sandstone canyon and entered the Rose-Red City of Petra back in *The Last Crusade* in 1989 it's topped most adventure-lovers must-visit travel lists. To see it on the big screen is one thing, but to visit it in person is quite something else.

It's just so very unlikely. Nestled deep in the Jordanian desert, hemmed in by sandstone crags and approached along a mere slither of an unassuming canyon – like any other – suddenly an opening ahead reveals something that seems so out of place you'd swear you were hallucinating. For, between the two faces of rock, an ancient facade looms. And not a weathered, barely-there outline of something great that once

was and has now been lost to time. This is a crisply-defined colossus of a frontage, six mighty pillars guarding the entrance as if the Nabateans (who built them two millennia ago) had just popped out for lunch. You gawp. You smile. You take the obligatory photo of the Treasury (for that's what it was) peeping out from the walls of the siq.

And that's just the start. Beyond this, the most iconic of the landmarks, is a sprawling collection of buildings, from a huge monastery to royal tombs, a classical theatre, a colonnaded Street and handfuls of small houses that appear suddenly in what on first glance appeared as nothing more than a blank wall of rock.

Once a major trading hub and home to no less than 30,000 people,

it's amazing to think that somewhere as impressive as this was ever 'lost' but it was. With the decline of the Nabatean civilization the entire settlement was forgotten by the west until, in 1812 it was rediscovered by a Swedish adventurer called Johann Burkhardt who was travelling disguised as an Arab.

You don't need much of an imagination to understand how he must have felt when he happened upon this place after spending so much time among the sandy deserts, because after taking the long and winding entranceway in – either by foot or by horse or camel – you'll experience that same sense of excitement and wonder, that same sense of discovering somewhere very special.

Then you find a quiet corner and contemplate the rock. You wax philosophical about mighty empires. You pinch yourself: you're in Petra.

MAKE IT HAPPEN: The best way to reach Petra is as part of an extended trip to Jordan. As both are in the south of the country, a perfect pairing is Wadi Rum and the Rose-Red City. In the former you can hire Bedouin guides and spend several days walking and camping on the sand surrounded by the naturally formed *jebels* (mountains) that mimic the man-made facades you'll see in Petra. For your visit to Petra itself, allow at least two days (or more). Go in the daytime to explore its furthest reaches, then consider going back at night when they line the way to the siq with candles.

9 TAKING A MOKORO THROUGH THE OKAVANGO DELTA, BOTSWANA

Sometimes what you can't see is more spine-tingling than what you can. So it is on a *mokoro* safari: hunkered down in the hull of a dugout canoe, you might be gliding through a green tunnel of reeds, but at any moment the mysterious plops, splashes and rustles could materialise into a hippo, a croc or – heart in mouth – an elephant, trunk dipped into water. But even when the megafauna are playing coy, the flash of a dazzling malachite kingfisher darting out from the reeds can be electrifying; you might also spot a jewel-like reed frog or a fish eagle perched nearby.

If you're prepared to hop out and hike for a while, you'll improve your chances of spotting bigger game: red lechwe, beautiful antelopes that splash through the shallows; a lounging lion or a leopard lolling on a branch; giraffe, hyena or even rare African wild dog.

Mostly, though, it's the serenity of the experience that's mesmerising, as you slip through the water punted along by your poler wielding his 3m-long *ngashi* pole. Traditionally carved from the trunk of an ebony or sausage tree, today *mokoro* are usually made from fibreglass – but they still provide the best way to explore the channels, lagoons, papyrus swamps and islands of the world's largest delta, spanning over 15,000 km sq.

MAKE IT HAPPEN: Maun is the gateway to the region. Pick up a tour there, or pre-book with a specialist operator. Moremi Game Reserve protects the eastern part of the delta, while private reserves offer luxury and opportunities for night drives and walking safaris.

8

EXPLORING BANFF NATIONAL PARK, CANADA

In the alpine-fun town of Banff, you can sit in the steamy hot springs on a chill winter's eve and thank the heavens that they were discovered here in the 1880s. It was these bubbling pools that first drew people to explore the mountains to the west of Calgary. Now most people come for those marvellous mountains themselves.

Banff is Canada's oldest national park, designated in 1885. But it's also perhaps the country's most classic protected place. Think of a cliché: giant snowy peaks, lakes of bright green-blue, wading moose, ambling bears, endless forests of sky-poking pine and spruce. Tick, tick, tick. Banff has all of these in spades. You can't find a wilderness that feels bigger, fresher, more intrinsically Canadian.

The park is a winner in winter or summer (and spring and autumn too). Skiers love the sheer scale of it, the flinty vistas spread out under the dome of a cobalt sky, clouds scudding along in orderly fashion. Oh, and the skiing, of course, which is perfect for novice and experienced skier alike – there are opportunities to both charge downhill or negotiate the backcountry.

Spring sees wildflowers fleck the meadows and snow-melt fill the rivers, before summer's full bloom – now the mountains will be full of hikers keen to bag summits, kip out in wood cabins and take day-strolls by mirror-still lakes – an excellent trail system makes anything possible. Summer is also the best season to drive down the Icefields Parkway, a contender for world's best

road. This stretch of tarmac is flanked by mountains, raging rivers, glittering lakes and the dazzling tongues of myriad glaciers – trips in specialised trucks allow you to drive right on the ice. There are innumerable tempting detours too, which might lead to quiet meadows and breathtaking lookouts, or even sightings of the mighty brown bear. In autumn, patches of forest flush with fall colour and the snow clouds begin to form – ready for the whole wonderful cycle to start all over again.

MAKE IT HAPPEN: A great way to get to this region (and explore more of Canada in the process) is to fly into Vancouver and then take the Rocky Mountaineer train, a two-day journey east to Banff. Go to www.rockymountaineer.com.

7 RIDING THE TRANS-SIBERIAN RAILWAY, RUSSIA

Six nights. 9,259km. Seven time zones. Millions upon millions of birch trees... A ride aboard the Trans-Siberian Railway is a head-spinning experience on many levels, not least because spending seven solid days on a train is enough to disorientate anyone.

Which is why few people do – spend seven consecutive days aboard, that is. Between the onion-domed churches of Moscow and the mountainous bays of Vladivostok, there are many reasons to hop off and explore, and not just because you need a change in cabin companions. There's Perm and Yekaterinburg, providing access to the rugged Ural Mountains. Irkutsk is worth a stroll to admire its neo-classical architecture, and is the gateway to Lake Baikal – the world's deepest lake, some 25 million years old and with a breathtakingly beautiful backdrop of mountains. To the south-east of the lake, Ulan-Ude offers a taste of Mongolian culture before the final haul to the coast of the Sea of Japan and Vladivostok.

That's the Trans-Siberian – but perhaps not what you meant? Many travellers choose instead to end their journey in Beijing, veering south from Ulan-Ude on the Trans-Mongolian via Ulan Bator, stopping-off point for excursions into the wild steppe, or the Trans-Manchurian through Harbin.

Whichever route you choose, you'll experience the vastness of Siberia, with its seemingly endless birch forests, and make new friends over a bottle (or five) of vodka. *Za zdarovye*!

MAKE IT HAPPEN: Most European travellers head east from Moscow – partly because starting with a train journey through Europe is romantic. The most popular season is May-September, though trains are well heated in winter. Book tickets and visas well in advance – for detailed planning advice visit www.seat61.com

6
LOOKING OUT FOR
BEARS, CANADA

Never mind going down to the woods today – if it's a bevy of picnicking bears you're after, Canada's undoubtedly your best option. From the creamy-white polar, to the hefty grizzly, the smaller black and even the rare spirit – there really is nowhere better for an ursine encounter. In fact it will be more of a case of picking which species tops your list.

If you're after polar bear sightings then you should head to Churchill, Manitoba, between October-November. Here you can take a tundra buggy to drive you close to the Arctic animals. Watch in awe as these curious (and hungry) bears approach your vehicle, then prepare to gasp as they jump up on their hind legs to get a better look at you as you attempt to take their

photograph. For a less crowded option you can also head to less-known Nunavik, Quebec's gorgeously wild Arctic wonderland and take a boat to get up close to these bewitching bears.

Those wanting a close encounter with grizzlies – a hefty sub-species of the brown bear – should head west to British Columbia. Here, beasts weighing up to 450kg can be seen in the mountains or, come salmon-spawning season (September-November), standing in crowds, mid-river, mouths open, waiting for lunch to jump right in. It's a truly incredible sight to behold – from a safe distance of course.

Another special treat is an encounter with the rare blonde-furred spirit bear (also called the Kermode bear). This rare sub-type inhabits the vast Great

Bear Rainforest – a remote thick woodland that spans between British Columbia's coast and south Alaska. Its distinctly coloured coat and the effort required to see it makes any encounter special. It's not surprising that the province of BC made it their official mammal and you won't be surprised to learn that it holds a special place in Native Indian legend, being the subject of many oral traditions.

MAKE IT HAPPEN: Generally, May-October is best for bear-watching. If camping in bear country it's vital you remain bear aware and obey the rules: clear up rubbish, keep food and toiletries in a bear locker or specially approved container, never approach a bear and, if walking, make noise as you go so as not to surprise them.

5 CROSSING THE SALAR DE UYUNI SALT FLATS, BOLIVIA

Geological marvel or one vast optical illusion? Whichever, the unique landscape of the world's largest salt flats in the south-west corner of Bolivia is a photographer's dream. The flatness and the colours and the down-right oddness seem to do strange things to your brain here – all sense of perspective can be lost; distance becomes impossible to measure. All that seems to exist is you, the sky and an endless crunch of blinding white.

The Salar de Uyuni is the leftovers of a scatter of prehistoric lakes, perched up at around 3,650m above sea level. It is breathtaking in all senses of the word. In the dry season these vast expanses appear as an endless patchwork of interlocking hexagonal shapes, white as the Arctic; in the rainy season (December to April), when the briny crust is covered in a shallow puddle of water, the area becomes a 9,000 sq km mirror, giving the sensation of travelling across the sky. Where workers have harvested the literal salt of the earth, small pyramids of the precious grains pock the flats like mini mountains.

Exploring here is wonderfully weird. This seemingly featureless expanse is one of the main routes across the altiplano, so traversing the dazzling plain by jeep is the norm. You can stay the night too – there are hotels here made entirely out of salt (well, there's little else to build from). The beds, chairs, tables, the lot – all carved from blocks of the white stuff, with a few scatter cushions for extra comfort.

There are 'sights' to visit. For instance, you can go to the rusting train graveyard around the town of Uyuni, where tracks built by the British at the end of the 19th century rust alongside old locos used for mining up until the 1940s. You can also bathe in steaming hot springs near the Chilean border, and visit pink flamingo breeding grounds at blood-red Laguna Colorada – the leggy birds love to tuck into the vibrant algae. But the main beauty of the Salar is being part of a landscape so very surreal.

MAKE IT HAPPEN: The hub-town of Uyuni is a seven-hour bus ride from Potosí; 12-15 hours by bus from capital La Paz. The seven-hour train ride from Oruro is a scenic access option. Tours out onto the Salar (the best, and safest, way to explore) can be arranged in Uyuni.

4
JAGUAR-SPOTTING IN THE
PANTANAL, **BRAZIL**

The Amazon has the size and the famous name, but it's in the Pantanal – Brazil's lesser-known great green wilderness – that you are more likely to meet the residents.

Indeed, a lot lives in this vast wetland. *A lot.* There are caiman skulking in the channels; there are capybara – the word's largest rodent, the size of a sheep — grazing on the grass; squirrel-sized marmosets bound about the bushes; giant otters crack crabs with their huge teeth; vast water lilies float like emerald coracles; and umpteen species of birds – egrets and storks, snail kites and kingfishers, hyacinth macaws and iridescent hummingbirds – fly amid it all. Indeed, so numerous are the avian species that you shouldn't expect to get too much

sleep – dawn here is less a tuneful chorus that a raucous cacophony.

However, perhaps the Pantanal's most sought-after sighting is the jaguar. And, unusually for this incredibly elusive cat, in the Pantanal they are regularly spotted. Stories abound of the beautiful rosette-splotched creatures posing on the riverbanks, in broad daylight, as if eager to be the stars of this tremendous show.

Simply driving along the road through the region, the Transpantaneira, can yield excellent wildlife sightings, while stays at a lodge within the *pantano* (swamp) will deliver a cawing, roaring, chirruping onslaught. However, it is at the very end of that road that sightings are usually most spectacular – this is known as 'jaguar central'.

Hop on a boat here to plunge down a channel off the Cuiabá River, keeping your eyes peeled. As your prow breaks the water weeds and the early-morning mist, and as the canopy thrums with skittering iguana, swinging monkeys and an encyclopedia of birds, you might just spy the sleek, spotted pelt of an enormous cat lazing by the water's edge, and gazing back at you with unconcerned amber eyes. A jaguar allowing you a privileged glimpse, and asserting its place as king of the wetland.

MAKE IT HAPPEN: In the north, the Transpantaneira Highway runs for 145km from Poconé (near Cuibá) to Porto Jofre; Campo Grande is the main access point for the southern areas of the Pantanal.

3

GAWPING AT THE
GRAND CANYON, USA

Not surprisingly, Arizona's world-beating Grand Canyon – up to 29km wide and 1.6km deep – is often voted one the greatest travel experiences: visitors can climb it, hike it, raft it, fly over it or simply palpitate on the edge of it, consumed by the ineffable geological scale.

Most people head to the South Rim where the crowds – in the summer at least – tend to take the sheen off the experience. Much better to head to the North Rim and then spend a couple of days hiking to the South Rim, taking in the buttes, mesas and stone outcrops along the way, sinking into the 'deep time' contained within its kaleidoscopic strata of rock.

MAKE IT HAPPEN: The Canyon is accessed via the nearby cities of Las Vegas (approx 450km) and Phoenix (370km). Plane and helicopter sightseeing trips leave from these hubs; otherwise expect a four- to six-hour drive, depending on which Rim you're aiming for. Private cars must pay a $30 entrance fee. www.nps.gov/grca.

2

SITTING AMONG
100,000 KING PENGUINS,
SOUTH GEORGIA

Any trip to this stupendously beautiful island starts with anticipation. Strewn out in the South Atlantic Ocean, over 1,000km from the Falklands there's no quick way to get here – it takes several days at sea.

First the colourful houses of the Argentine outpost of Ushuaia disappear along with the rest of the South American continent, then the green fingers of land slip away into the sea. Once out on the open water, giant seabirds begin to hover and circle above your vessel – giant petrels, black-browed albatross and sooty shearwaters. Until finally, after a brief stop at the Falklands, you reach a cluster of guano-covered atolls known as Shag Rocks which mark the tip of South Georgia.

Your first landing will begin with a smell. A not-too-unpleasant but never to be forgotten ammonia-tinged scent than reaches you way before your Zodiac lands on the beach. You'll spy giant boulders on the shore but, as you move closer, they'll begin to move and you'll slowly realise that these aren't stationary objects at all but seals – hundreds of them. From the giant, flatulence-emitting but utterly adorable rounded elephant seals to the bluff-charging adolescent fur seals, whose pups are smaller than your boots and will try and sneak into your rucksack. You'll have to work to keep the regulated 5m from the creatures, as they won't have attended the same briefing, until, finally you spy the scene stealers – the harlequin painted king penguins.

First you'll see one, or maybe two – or perhaps be lucky enough to watch a trio of these waddling birds walking in a line, inexplicably slapping each other while locked in an intense gaze. You'll be mesmerized and then you'll hear it. A high-pitched wailing that sounds similar to wind tearing through a wire fence at high speed. Then prepare for sensory overload as crowds of tens of thousands of penguins appear ahead. Recent numbers at the famous Salisbury Plain, estimated 60,000 pairs – that's over 120,000 kings plus (depending on when you visit) their chicks crowding the vast beaches like an elaborate *Where's Wally?* picture.

The backdrop to this mind-blowing wild gathering is almost as spectacular – giant rising peaks yawning into the air with rugged and pointed summits between deep, scooped-out gorges filled with giant glaciers.

But it doesn't end there, South Georgia is where one of the most remarkable tales of survival ended – Shackleton's Endurance Expedition. After being blighted by sea ice, surviving perilous seas and crossing South Georgia's unexplored mountain chain, he finally reach help and safety at Stromness an old whaling station in 1916. A lover of this island, his grave sits in Grytviken where you can toast his – and your own – southern adventure.

MAKE IT HAPPEN: Most expedition cruises that leave from Ushuaia (Argentina) head straight to the Antarctica, look for one that takes in South Georgia too.

1 CRUISING THE GALÁPAGOS ISLANDS, ECUADOR

On this unique, remote archipelago in the Pacific, 1,000km west of mainland Ecuador, the animals have never learned fear of man. They ignore the captivated visitors and simply get on with their daily business. Every island has a completely different atmosphere, different landscape and different species. One day you're watching giant tortoises mate in swirling highland mists, the next you're nose-to-nose with a seafaring lizard, the next you're snorkelling with a group of penguins... on the equator.

And, as Darwin came to appreciate, neighbouring islands have sub-species that have evolved differently, leading to one of the most important, world-changing discoveries ever known. In short, scientifically, scenically and sensorially spectacular.

MAKE IT HAPPEN: The best way to explore is by boat. Although three or four night cruises are available, try to go for a week at least.

THE 100 GREATEST TRAVEL EXPERIENCES TICKLIST

SO, THERE'S THE FINAL COUNTDOWN – A FEET-ITCHING MIX OF ANIMAL ENCOUNTERS, MOUNTAIN CLIMBS AND SUPER SITES. BUT HOW MANY HAVE YOU DONE?

100	Machu Picchu/Inca Trail, **Peru**	☐
99	Halong Bay, **Vietnam**	☐
98	Karakoram Highway, **Pakistan**	☐
97	Stromboli, **Italy**	☐
96	Polar bears, Spitsbergen, **Norway**	☐
95	Uluru at sunrise/sunset, **Australia**	☐
94	Kyoto, **Japan**	☐
93	Getting lost in Venice, **Italy**	☐
92	Husky sledding, **Sweden**	☐
91	Wadi Rum under the stars, **Jordan**	☐
90	Iguaçu Falls, **Argentina/Brazil**	☐
89	InterRailing, **Europe, Various**	☐
88	Jokhang & Potala Palace, **Tibet/China**	☐
87	Lemurs, **Madagascar**	☐
86	Alaska's wilderness, **USA**	☐
85	The Ganges, **India**	☐
84	Isfahan, **Iran**	☐
83	Tongariro Crossing, **New Zealand**	☐
82	Sossusvlei, **Namibia**	☐
81	Hoi An, **Vietnam**	☐
80	Etosha NP, **Namibia**	☐
79	Whalewatching, Québec, **Canada**	☐
78	Taman Negara NP, **Malaysia**	☐
77	Diving, Great Barrier Reef, **Australia**	☐
76	Tikal, **Guatemala**	☐
75	Yellowstone NP, **USA**	☐
74	Boat along the Mekong, **Laos**	☐
73	Franz Josef Glacier, **New Zealand**	☐
72	Skeleton Coast from the air, **Namibia**	☐
71	Kayaking, Fiordland, **New Zealand**	☐
70	Motorcycle/bike ride, **Vietnam**	☐
69	Rome & Vatican City, **Italy**	☐
68	Gorilla watching, **Rwanda/Uganda**	☐
67	Sigiriya, **Sri Lanka**	☐
66	Backpacking, **Australia**	☐
65	Hampi, **India**	☐
64	Perito Moreno Glacier, **Argentina**	☐
63	Yosemite NP, **USA**	☐
62	Keralan backwaters, **India**	☐
61	Rafting the Zambezi, **Zambia**	☐
60	Angkor Wat, **Cambodia**	☐
59	Angel Falls, **Venezuela**	☐
58	Fraser Island, **Australia**	☐
57	Kathmandu backstreets, **Nepal**	☐
56	Salsa & mojitos, Havana, **Cuba**	☐
55	New York City, **USA**	☐
54	Atacama & El Tatio geysers, **Chile**	☐
53	Diving Caye Caulker, **Belize**	☐
52	Pyramids of Meroë, **Sudan**	☐
51	Road-tripping, **USA**	☐

50	Himalaya, **Bhutan/India**	☐
49	Bush safari, **Botswana**	☐
48	Lake Titicaca, **Peru**	☐
47	Victoria Falls, **Zambia/Zimbabwe**	☐
46	Royal Chitwan NP, **Nepal**	☐
45	Easter Island moai, **Chile**	☐
44	Old Cartagena, **Colombia**	☐
43	Rhinos, **Swaziland**	☐
42	Torres del Paine, **Chile**	☐
41	Cenote diving, Yucatán, **Mexico**	☐
40	Whale & dolphin watching, **New Zealand**	☐
39	Cappadocia, **Turkey**	☐
38	Elephants, Addo Elephant NP, **South Africa**	☐
37	Visiting Auschwitz, **Poland**	☐
36	Outer Hebrides, **Scotland**	☐
35	Bagan, **Burma**	☐
34	Sydney Harbour Bridge, **Australia**	☐
33	Mount Everest, **Nepal**	☐
32	Falkland Islands, **Falkland Islands**	☐
31	Orangutans, Borneo, **Malaysia & Indonesia**	☐
30	Temples of Abu Simbel, **Egypt**	☐
29	Taj Mahal, **India**	☐
28	Tiger's Nest Monastery, **Bhutan**	☐
27	Whitewater rafting, **Nepal**	☐
26	Solar eclipse, **Various**	☐
25	Zanzibar, **Tanzania**	☐
24	Utah's canyons, **USA**	☐
23	Perhentian/Tioman Islands, **Malaysia**	☐
22	South Luangwa NP, **Zambia**	☐
21	Kakadu NP, **Australia**	☐
20	Santorini, **Greece**	☐
19	Northern lights, **Various**	☐
18	Table Mountain, **South Africa**	☐
17	Milford Sound, **New Zealand**	☐
16	Walking the Great Wall, **China**	☐
15	Snorkelling with rays, Bora Bora, **French Polynesia**	☐
14	Masai Mara/Serengeti safari, **Kenya/Tanzania**	☐
13	Kilimanjaro, **Tanzania**	☐
12	Sea kayaking with orca, **Canada**	☐
11	Antarctica, **Antarctica**	☐
10	Petra, **Jordan**	☐
9	Okavango Delta, **Botswana**	☐
8	Banff NP, **Canada**	☐
7	Trans-Siberian Railway, **Russia**	☐
6	Bear watching, **Canada**	☐
5	Salar de Uyuni, **Bolivia**	☐
4	Jaguar spotting, Pantanal, **Brazil**	☐
3	Grand Canyon, **USA**	☐
2	King penguins, **South Georgia**	☐
1	Galápagos Islands, **Ecuador**	☐